Dear Doctor
I am your teacher…

MARY JANE HOLT

Warmly and Respectfully
Dedicated

To the nurse healers and teachers in the trenches
who are fighting, winning, and knowing they matter
and that they absolutely can, and must, and do
make a difference every day.

Dear Doctor, I am your teacher…

Saturday, October 15, 2005

Dear Doctor:

I am more than your diagnosis. I am more than a virus. I am more than any acute or chronic disease. I am more than lung or breast or brain cancer. I am more than any tumor — malignant or benign. I am more than a near fatal accident. I am more than any injury. I am more than a stroke, or a heart attack, or a hot gall bladder. I am more than a failed organ. I am more than a stomach-ache, an earache, or a sore throat. I am more than a classic depression or a panic disorder. I am more than a sum of difficult or minor symptoms. I am more than a room number. I am more than a case file. I am more than a good paying insurance patient, or an indigent waste of your valuable time.

I am so much more. I want you to know there are people who love me. I need you to be aware that there are those whose lives are enriched because I am a part of those lives. I am a big deal. I often require more of you than surgery or prescriptions alone. I need you to hear me, to listen to me, to observe me. I am your teacher. I always have been your teacher. I forever will be.

We are a team — you and me. Without me you are nothing. Without you... well, sometimes, I might still survive!

Sincerely,

Your Patient

Dear Doctor, I am your teacher...

In Her Embrace

in her embrace
I sigh
inside I die
for I know anger
and she knows me
my constant companion
she
but I shall be
one day free
of the prison
her hands hath made
because I stayed
deceitful her ways
necessary she says
to protect me...
I'd as soon be dead!
or in her arms I die
a little each day
her chains choking me
cutting off my breath
like death
though I do not forget
how once I sighed
in her embrace

mjh

Dear Doctor, I am your teacher…

Anger can keep you alive – for a time – when nothing else can. Sadly, many individuals become so consumed with anger that its powerful flame destroys the essence of who they are, leaving behind an empty, blackened, desecrated and unforgiving soul in which compassion, understanding, gratitude and forgiveness never can live again. I am among the lucky ones whose unforgiving soul was not destroyed by the fire of anger. I am most blessed. "Dear Doctor, I am your teacher" is part of my medical (hi)STORY.

This manuscript is nearly 20 years old. I wrote it privately and primarily for my own therapy. Over the years, I have read it again and again to remind myself that I am a survivor. I finally and somewhat reluctantly share it now because there have been Lessons Learned that may enable you to be a survivor, too, in these trying times.

I hope so.

- mjh

ACKNOWLEDGMENTS

It's not possible to name all the nurses and doctors and countless other health professionals who have influenced my life, even saved my life, more than once. Nor could I ever name all the patients whose stories inspire my heart to beat with gratitude because they let me walk a ways with them. I must simply acknowledge that I am blessed by all.

The Battle to Survive Begins

"You are just like all my other nurse patients. Nurses are horrible patients. You think you have to tell us what to do. I am the doctor, and you are the patient. You are supposed to tell me how you feel, not what to do. I decide that."

As the surgeon's words burned into my soul, I started to shrivel inside. Tears threatened. Some voice within my body, that I did not recognize, whimpered weakly, "I feel bad. I am sick."

"Of course you feel bad." Dr. A continued, "You just had major surgery six days ago. You are not going to feel better until you are out of here. All you can do is find fault with this hospital. You are just like my husband who griped and complained about a light that would not work while he was a patient at another hospital."

My sister, ever the eager one over the previous 24 hours to do exactly what the doctor was suggesting, asked, "Well, can I take her home, right now? Today?"

"No" responded the surgeon, "she needs to stay one more day. She can go tomorrow."

I believed that doctor. I believed I was a horrible patient. I believed I was just like all other nurses who were bad patients. I believed I was a complainer, that nothing could please me. I immediately did not like the person I suddenly lay in that hospital bed believing myself to be. In reality, I was anything and everything but such a description. I would not remember the truth about who I was, and am, for many very long months. It would be more than two years before I could begin to say with some degree of confidence, "I am somebody worthy of life and health – worthy of caring and being cared for!"

Lesson Learned

"First, do no harm…" means exactly what it says.

Inspiration

On Saturday, October 15, 2005, Gwyn Hyman Rubio, the author of *Icy Sparks* and *The Woodsman's Daughter*, inspired me to record this story. She encouraged me to lay out the facts - to be straightforward. Somehow, she made me believe I could do it. Many others had tried, but it was she who convinced me that sharing the facts, as I knew them, truly could help others, as well as myself. Her most recent novel when we met, *The Woodsman's Daughter*, had made me aware that she knew about the grey room. Talking with her had confirmed that she knew a lot about it. She said others go there, too, and sometimes they cannot find their way back out. She even led me to believe that perhaps my story could help keep folks from ever entering that grey/black room full of nothingness. It is, indeed, a room like none other from which there occasionally can be no escape.

One chance meeting followed by a ninety-minute phone conversation, and I knew I had found someone who completely understood where I had come from. She knew the importance of being true not only to one's calling in life, but to the very essence of who we are and where we come from. Clearly, she made the point that only when our truth escapes from the springboard of honest and personal reality is it believable. "I do it through fiction," she said, "you may have to write this one as a memoir."

"But what will I do with the anger?" I wondered aloud. "I do not want anything I might choose to share to be all about anger. Also, I would not want this to be just a memoir — it would have to be self-help, as well."

"Your story is what it is. Anger can be good," she said.

Suddenly, I realized anew that anger, like so many other negatively perceived emotions, can be useful. It is all in how we use such emotions, as well as how we guard against being used by them.

"You can do this," she said, "you should do this. The tone in which you do it will make all the difference. You are a good writer." Gwyn, a gifted writing teacher, encouraged me to honor whatever tone might demand to be heard if I chose to share the facts. She said it was okay if the tones changed in nonfiction. She seemed to believe strongly that there was a potential for helping others through my effort.

"But I would want to be fair to the doctor," is what I heard myself saying to Gwyn once we were past the anger and tone discussion. I could hardly believe my words. For three years, I had felt many things toward and about Dr. A, but a desire to be fair to her had never entered my conscious mind. I told Gwyn how I had awakened on a Sunday morning only a few months prior to our conversation, and how my very first thought had been, "You can forgive her now." I immediately knew who the "her" was in this strange consideration that had come to me so suddenly that morning. I asked my unconscious mind "Why?"

"Because you can travel lighter if you do," came the answer as clearly as any communication I have ever received from any source. I chose not to act immediately, however, on the permission given to me by inner self/heart/mind that morning.

Following that first lengthy conversation with Gwyn, I silently replayed my words, "But I want to be fair to the doctor." Yep, I had said them. Aloud. I would soon realize they were true.

I have lived my entire life wanting to be fair to everybody – wanting to understand all sides. I suppose I was somewhat relieved to hear those words come out of my mouth. Suddenly I realized that the anger no longer ruled. Perhaps I could be fair. Perhaps I really could tell my story, the whole of it – in part… Perhaps I also could eventually forgive.

Later, my sister's words echoed Gwyn's, "She's right. You need to be more personal. People want to know your story. Your truth."

"But what if I cannot tell it? What if I do not have the courage?" I wondered. ("Of course, you have the courage to tell your story," Gwyn had said.) "I'm not sure I can do this. What if I just cannot see it through?" I asked my sister.

"Then do it, or do not do it. It's your choice. Either way is fine," was my sister's response.

Choice

To tell or not to tell my story was, and is, indeed, my choice. Suddenly, I realized I had many choices. For a time, I'd had little or no choice at all regarding the events of the fall and winter of 2002/2003. Without my invitation, or even my permission, those few months had become a defining period of my life. They were what they were.

Today, I am what I am. I will make the choices now about how I will use that defining period and the influences that came with it. I am so much more than what I allowed those events to inspire me to become for a while.

Inspiration can come from both positive and negative sources. Then, regardless of the source, inspiration can be received positively or negatively. In fact, inspiration can come from anything, anyone, any set of circumstances. Inspiration is what it is. What we do with our inspiration is frequently a matter of choice.

Inspiration is most often positively considered

synonymous with motivation, stimulation, or
encouragement. ████████████████ are often
believed to be o████████████inspiration can
come over a long████████or in a flash. We
may feel that we have████████in the heat of the
moment. Perhaps, amid████████or disaster, that is how
heroes are born. Artists, writers, and all creative types
may be inspired in an instant or over a lifetime.

Evildoers, killers, murderers, thieves, rapists have
their inspirations, too. The source of inspiration
often can be the same for individuals, small groups, or
throngs of people. While the source is the same,
perception will vary. Responses to the source of that
inspiration, or to the inspiring words or actions
emanating from that common source, are myriad.
What motivates or encourages one often spells clear
defeat for another. Choice always plays a part in the
difference between victory and defeat.

Anger has played a tremendous role in my being able
to reach this point today where I eagerly turn to my
keyboard and now welcome the words that I know
are ready to come. I invite these very welcome words
to fall where they may.

At this writing, it has been three years and two
months and the anger is still with me. I do not want
to be angry anymore. With a sincere prayer in my
heart for guidance, I trust that this keyboard exercise
will help to cleanse me of not only the unhealthy

aspects of anger, but all other negative emotions, as well, concerning the events of the fall and winter of 2002/2003.

Exposure

There are corners of our hearts where pain hides, pain which emanates from a few almost forgotten memories, memories hidden well beneath life's surface. Then, one day Courage comes walking into the present moment with an offer to lead the way into the past. He carries a strange Light designed to expose the hidden thoughts of the heart. Courage knows exposure will bring Victory. Victory will be accompanied by Freedom and only those willing to risk the journey will come to know Freedom well. As the Light of Courage shines into our hearts it slowly penetrates every area where old emotional debris has been harbored over the year. In His wisdom, God allows circumstances to come our way which sometimes cause us to recoil. Suppression is a mechanism which frequently is used when life becomes a bit too painful. And, yes, I suppose we can take to the grave a whole lifetime of suppressed memories...

But, what a waste.
To have had such events take so much from us
it seems only fair that they give something back.

I believe God works in myriad ways and sometimes it is on the journey backward or inward where He is found in all His sufficiency. Occasionally, it is in seeking to know ourselves that we come to know Him. We are His creation, made in His image and He has a vested interest in us. In sincerely desiring with all our hearts, to know Him and in never giving up the quest, Victory comes, Truth is revealed and Freedom for all eternity becomes ours. Sometimes, it is a fragrance, or a sunset, or the feel of a brisk and refreshing wind on a scorching summer day which triggers the first memory. As it surfaces, fear may knock, wanting to come in for one last visit. Do not give entrance. Let Courage lead and let His light shine, for His penetrating beams will enable you to see how to clean house. Joy will knock shortly and Laughter lies just around the bend. Make way. Prepare for their visit. Perhaps they will stay a while...

Surviving

I had always been a survivor. I win my battles. There simply had never been any other option. Oh, there may have been a quickly passing thought of permanently escaping the misery of my first heartbreak. And once, when I was very physically ill, it had occurred to me in one extraordinarily fleeting instant that I could put an end to my misery. Other than those two very brief (momentary) occasions prior to 2002, I do not recall ever having entertained thoughts about taking my own life. Certainly, I had never prayed and asked God to please let me die.

I had witnessed my first death at age two. It was an occasion of mixed emotion, lots of hugging and laughing and crying… and good food. I vividly recall toddling around and being able to see under the hospital bed in which my young cousin William lay in the corner of the room. I remember the warmth of the mammoth fireplace in my aunt Grace's home. I could not see the food, but I could see others helping themselves to it. It was a good day. I was cradled in the bosom of my mama's family. No matter what happened, I was safe, and I knew it. Thus, William's death did not tragically scar me for life. Not at all. It taught me at a very young age that death and life walked hand in hand, as did joy and grief, laughter, and tears … and good food.

Shortly after William's death, I developed whooping

cough. I remember it well. I have had asthma issues ever since. My preschool years were laced with hospitalizations, oxygen tents, antibiotics, and drugs, drugs and more drugs that caused me to shake and tremble and go without sleep.

I remember when I was five years old, and a nurse came to stick my cold finger that was tucked inside the oxygen tent where I was struggling to breathe. She had stuck me every day for three days. I said no. She pleaded. I adamantly said no. She said she would have to call the doctor. I said, "Call him then, and tell him if you don't stick me today that I will let you stick me tomorrow and I won't even cry." The doctor said that sounded like a deal. I've never cried since because of a needle and there have been lots of needles.

To this day, my sister, Lynda, swears that all my grown-up ailments are somehow tied to those awful drugs that enabled me to keep breathing, and thus living through my early years. At age thirteen, our family doctor told my folks I would not live to be thirty because of all the strain on my heart, caused, he said, by both the severe asthma, the medication side effects, and my extreme sensitivity to so many medications.

Later, another physician in a town to which we relocated, would try to convince me, at age 17, to become a nurse. "You would make a perfect nurse," he said, "you could be a healer." I had no interest in becoming a nurse. A healer? Maybe. A nurse? No way.

Way, however, would lead to way, and by the fall of 1966, I had enrolled in a practical nursing program. "Just to have some kind of degree to use to work my way through journalism school in the future" is what I told myself. The future, as it turned out, arranged for me to meet my husband-to-be on the night I graduated from that nursing program.

Marriage and children followed. And more ill health. At age 23, I was told that I would not live another five years if I did not quit smoking. Considering how sick I was, and how hard I was once more struggling just to breathe and keep living…, giving up cigarettes may have been easy enough to do at the time – if I had ever smoked. I never had. But my dad had. And my husband had. And many friends. And their secondhand smoke had embedded itself into the linings of my lungs, destroying the delicate low-lying tissue of my bronchioles (tiny airways within the lungs). My past medical history and two decades of secondhand smoke exposure had set me up for a diagnosis of bronchiectasis. (Bronchiectasis is an abnormal stretching and enlarging of the respiratory passages caused by mucus blockage. When the body is unable to get rid of mucus, mucus becomes stuck and accumulates in the airways. The blockage and accompanying infection cause inflammation, leading to the weakening and widening of the passages. The weakened passages can become scarred and deformed, allowing more mucus and bacteria to accumulate, resulting in a cycle of infection and blocked airways. (SOURCE – American Lung Association). Of course, I already knew much too well what bronchiectasis was all about. I had watched my mom hemorrhage countless times and experience innumerable hospitalizations through the years because of her bronchiectasis. I would have no part of such a diagnosis. I refused it.

"How can I get well?" I asked the confused thoracic surgeon who had just told me that, not only would I never be well again, but that I would never work as a nurse again, and that I should avoid crowds for the rest of my life, and that I would have good days and bad days, as well as weeks on antibiotics, and weeks off... "You will have to adjust," he said, as he left the room, adding that he would return with my prescriptions momentarily.

Then he went into the examining room next door to mine. He left my door standing open. He did not close the door of the room he entered. I knew what patient was in that room. I had seen the skinny old man come in. He had looked like walking death as he made his way into the office that morning. I listened closely.

"How was your trip?" the doctor asked.

"Great, really wonderful" weakly gasped the old man.

"He really had a good time!" said the female who accompanied him.

"Is there anything else you want to do before the end?" the doctor asked.

The end? He really is at death's door, I thought to myself. And the doctor is asking him if there is anything else he wants to DO before the end! How dare he? After sitting in my room lecturing to me about all I cannot do, he goes into the next room and talks to a fellow who really is dying and asks what else he still wants to DO.

Sweet rebellious anger burned. Good, healthy anger. "We will just see about this situation," I said to myself.

When the surgeon returned to my room with prescriptions in hand, I repeated, "What can I do to get well?"

"Have you not heard a word I have said?" He responded.

"I heard you. Every word. And I heard what you said to the man next door, too. I do not want to start getting ready to die. I want to live. I want to get well and there are lots of things I want to DO. So, give me a best-case scenario. Just suppose I can get well. What would I have to do to make that happen? What would be my part in the effort?"

Reluctantly, very reluctantly, he began outlining my best-case scenario. I left his office that day, resolved to take as directed all the pills he prescribed: the antibiotics, the steroids, the bronchodilators, the phenobarbital to help with the horrible shaking and the rapid heartbeat… Yep, I would take his pills and I would faithfully do the postural drainage (hang off my bed from the waist, for several minutes, several times a day). No one would ever smoke a cigarette in my home or automobile again. And I would do what only I could do which was to stay focused on my future.

It would be a productive, happy future in which I would do all the things I wanted to do every day that I lived. I would not wait until I really was dying before resolving to do that, and if this doctor, whom I liked a lot and sincerely respected, thought I was dying already – well, he had another thought coming. Together, he and I would be a team. It did not matter if he did not believe. For the time being, I had enough fight in me for both of us. Enough faith. Enough determination.

By the following summer, I was able to work for three months on the mental health unit at a nearby hospital. Granted, I did not go back to my profession in the middle of flu season, nor to a medical floor in a hospital, but I went back to some semblance of my previous life and to my nursing identity.

A couple of years later, after surviving two automobile accidents, I began to work part time at my sons' pediatrician's office. I did a little private duty at area hospitals and a bit of volunteer work in hospital settings, as well. Around 1980, I discovered the perfect place for me – the nurse in me, that is – in a family practice office. There, I became part of a team that cared for not only the whole person, but the whole family. I had just begun to come into my own when a malfunctioning thyroid started to interfere with my near perfect life. I will not bore you with all the details of the thyroid disease, or the gall bladder disease that resulted in a major old fashioned cholecystectomy surgery by 1984. The developing symptoms, medication side effects and surgical complications are unimportant just now except to say that the cards continued to be stacked against the survival of my colon.

Willful Identity Change

I chose to leave nursing in 1986 because I wanted to write. At first, it was just going to be a sabbatical. I needed to write to heal a few emotional wounds I was carrying at the time. My intentions were to return to the clinical setting within six months, a year at most.

Once more, way would lead to way, and I never went back. As it turned out, my 18 years of nursing had proven to be the perfect school of journalism for the kind of writing I wanted to do.

I quickly came to realize that I personally could do more to address what I had come to call the "pain behind the pain" with my pen, than I could using the tools the nursing profession had provided to me.

In February of 1988, I launched a little monthly magazine that I called The Community Health Focus. It was the first effort of its kind in my state. I had heard of something called "managed care" that was about to drastically change health care as Americans had known it for several decades.

In fact, I had caught a fleeting clinical glimpse of the actual face of mis-managed care just prior to leaving nursing. I strongly felt that the public needed to be better educated in all things health related, so I wanted to do my part to make that happen.

Shortly after the launch of my local magazine, area

television stations began offering regular prime time health news and education coverage. I personally telephoned several major newspaper editors around the state and urged them to find ways to provide more health education and offer more health news coverage.

I reckon I had found a need or hit a nerve. Awards started coming my way. I did not seek them. I do not enter contests. I am not a joiner. My life as a writer requires solitude. When I choose to spend time with an individual or in a crowd, I tend to choose wisely. I must do this because I am a sponge. I absorb the emotions of almost everybody with whom I come in contact.

It always has been that way. I like me like I am. Otherwise I probably would have sought to change. Being sponge-like has served well the writer in me. My body, however, has taken the brunt of much of the emotion I have absorbed.

While my heart and soul wept and soared with the lives and deaths of so many individuals I have come to know and love well, my physical shell, or earth suit, as I sometimes call it, paid a price. My colon was the first organ to totally fail.

At this writing, no one can offer conclusive reasons as to why colonic inertia develops. Clearly, in my case there were many precipitating factors. Antihistamines

since infancy for all my allergies; the gall bladder
surgery and resulting adhesions which had certainly
slowed peristalsis (bowel contraction/mobility) and
left me continuously constipated; the thyroid disease;
and yes, the burden of carrying around so many
emotions within myself – all this and more may have
played a role.

Lesson Learned

I made a conscious decision at one point to never say, "My gut tells me…" anything. I do not say phrases like "My heart breaks…" or "My head is killing me…" I learned over time, but not in time. I encourage you to do the same. I will explain more later.

The Perfect Surgeon?

By the late 1990's, I consulted a doctor who I perceived to be the perfect surgeon. Dr. A came highly recommended. When I met her, the first thing I noticed was her tiny hands. How awesome, I thought it would be, if every surgeon could have tiny, capable hands. At our very first encounter, it was clear to me that she was all-surgeon. In fact, she prefaced several of her comments with "I am a surgeon…" Her answer, as a surgeon, was to remove my colon. Her comment following her recommendation, however, was, "Of course, we do not know for sure, and may never know exactly, what has caused your colon to fail, so we have no way of knowing whether or not your small bowel will fail, as well."

That comment was enough for me to do more research. I tried acupuncture, deep tissue massage: full body and feet. Strangely, the foot massage – reflexology - was somewhat effective, but only for a while. During the nearly five years that I waited to finally accept the surgery, I became dependent on Milk of Magnesia and Fleets enemas to achieve any kind of relief. I was extremely miserable. And I was sick, very sick, when I finally went back to that surgeon, Dr. A, and said, "I'm ready."

In looking back – and oh, my, how different things do look in retrospect – it is clear to me now that the stage was already set for complications to arise. I was just too sick to see it happening. And the doctor, a focused and talented surgeon, apparently, ...at that point in time... either did not have, or did not practice, using the gifts and talents that a successful whole person physician and healer must or should use every day and with every patient.

Managed care had just forced a change in my primary care doctors. The new one did not know me well at all. Yet, he, Dr. B, proved to be detail oriented and a valuable source of support in the months and years following the surgery. But while my family and I were in the throes of crisis, we all felt lost. During those "lost" months/years..., I personally felt stuck in or near the doorway to an ugly grey room filled with pain, or something that I discovered was actually worse than pain, with Dr. A's words continually ringing in my brain, "You are just like all my other nurse patients. Nurses are horrible patients. You think you have to tell us what to do. I am the doctor. You are the patient. You are to tell me how you feel, not what to do. I decide that." The strong and mature fifty-four-year-old woman I was suddenly had turned into a lost little girl that I had never known before – one who would lose herself over and over before I would finally find me again. That cowardly and weak little girl's whimpering response to the surgeon: "I feel bad. I am sick," would rule the essence of who I was for a very long time.

Lesson Learned

Cruel and harshly spoken words have the potential for doing great damage to the heart, soul, and ultimately the body of us all.

Fair?

At this point, I will try to give those of you who require it more background. Perhaps these coming details will lead you to come to your own conclusions regarding what happened to me physically, emotionally, and spiritually… and why it happened. With a degree of reluctance, I share some of what I am about to share. Still, I now choose to be more open because, invariably at the end of each of my "You Are Somebody and I am, too!" workshops, participants always ask, "Where did this come from?"

I usually tell participants that the details of my story are not important. I say, "What is important is the way you use what I give to you."

Occasionally, someone will respond, "but that is not fair. We want to know about you."

Very rarely have I shared the details you are about the read. Yet, repeatedly, by both those who have heard some of the facts and those who have heard none, I have been told that the sharing of more of my truth can help others. Certainly, there was an exceptionally wise Man who said a very long time ago that the truth will set us free. Gwyn Hyman Rubio made me believe it could happen. I hope it will. I want to be free again.

Medical History

August 25, 2021, Update

This more extensive medical history which I am about to share is one reason I have held back on publishing this story for nearly 20 years. Many details are shared very reluctantly, but shared nevertheless, because it will give you a glimpse of what nurses deal with every single day. Doctors usually admit patients to the hospital for their present-day chief complaint and with a focus on the diagnosis of the hour. **Nurses then coordinate total care for the whole person behind that diagnosis of the hour and they must consider complex past histories as they do so.** *I think it is important for us to understand this and to know that many a nurse has saved many a doctor's ass (and license) time and time again!*

After I recovered from the complications of my colectomy, my primary care doctor suggested that I lecture at medical schools when I was stronger. He said there was much that doctors could learn from me. That was and is true, but not just true of me. Every patient has a history and is a story. Many of those stories are riddled with much more anguish and pain, and far more daily struggle than I have experienced.

I have dedicated my life to helping them tell their stories.
Now, with gratitude for their courage, I try to tell mine.

~ mjh

The Suture Allergy Discovery

In the fall of 1980, the discovery of lumps in both breasts required that bilateral breast biopsies be done. Following the surgery, my breasts were extremely tender and both sites had a great deal of drainage, far more than I and the doctor had expected they would have. The surgeon made comments about the inflammation and drainage being more than normal. We did not know why this was the case. I just know my breasts were sore for a very long time, and then, for years, I would develop frequent hives along the suture line.

Then, in the mid 1980's, I had the gall bladder surgery. I spent about two weeks in the hospital. I had asthma following the surgery, as well as chills and low-grade fever. I remained very tender for months following the procedure and once again experienced hives for years along the suture line, accompanied by what felt like major itching deep down inside. I do not know how to fully explain that, except now that I think about it, perhaps it could have been compared to the way my ears and eustachian tubes itch when I'm having an allergy attack. Still, today, I occasionally get hives along that long gall bladder surgical incision line.

Then, around 1993, a hysterectomy was required. When I returned for a recheck following the surgery, the doctor commented that it looked like I was having an internal, possibly "allergic like," reaction to the sutures she had used. She asked if I had ever had a suture reaction in the past.

Suddenly, it occurred to me that perhaps that was what had happened with the breast and gall bladder surgeries. I later discovered that the same type of suture had been used for all three surgeries. Vicryl and Dexon were the trade names, and I was told they are the same thing. It was made clear to me that I should never let that type of suture be used on me again.

In 1997, I needed to have still more surgery: repair work done for a cystocle (a fallen or unsupported bladder) and rectocele (a rectocele is usually described as a bulge or prolapse of the rectal wall into the vaginal space – resulting in a thinning or weakening of the rectal wall). Prior to this surgery, when I discussed the suture allergy with my gynecologist, he, Dr. C, and I felt like I should be tested for allergy to other sutures before we chose one to use in the repair. He applied samples of suture in three places on my body and two weeks later I exhibited what appeared to be an allergic reaction to two of the sutures, so we went with Monocryl, the one suture to which I did not react.

Dr. C used the Monocryl and I did not appear to have any kind of local reaction. However, about a month after surgery, I developed other allergy symptoms, including angioedema (dangerous swelling) of the face, lips and throat, and asthmatic wheezing. Since I knew the suture had probably started to be absorbed into my body at that point I was a bit nervous that the symptoms, which had been serious enough to warrant two ER visits, might have been caused by the suture; but, since the inflammatory/allergic type symptoms did not continue for any length of time as they had with other surgeries, I guessed that the sutures may not have been the culprit behind those episodes.

The Inevitable Colon Surgery

The First Appointment with Dr. A

Following my development of thyroid disease and gall
bladder surgery in the mid 1980's, I began
experiencing major constipation problems. For years,
following the instructions of my doctor, I took stool
softeners to aid in having a bowel movement. This on
top of having taken an antihistamine every day of my
life and living with the ever-present adhesions from
previous surgeries, led to the defecation (bowel
emptying) problem only growing worse over time. At
one point in the late 1990's, Dr. D, a
gastroenterologist, referred me to Dr. A for a
consultation. As I mentioned earlier, at that first visit,
Dr. A had communicated quite pragmatically, but
courteously, that what she could offer was a
colectomy, that is: removal of the colon. I actually
liked her communication style and thought she
listened well at my first appointment with her.

At that first visit, I discussed my concern about
further reaction to sutures. I recall vividly how she
said she would therefore use silk and titanium,
"because nobody ever reacts to them." I recall telling
her I was allergic to gold – that I could wear cheap
jewelry for short periods of time but had never been
able to wear gold. That doesn't matter, she said,
titanium is an inert material, and nobody will react to
it. We discussed my symptoms and suture allergy in

31

detail. (When I later requested a copy of my records from Dr. A's office, no notes from that first visit were included.)

Returning to Dr. A

Following that first consultation, I did not agree to surgery. As I already told you, I chose to try acupuncture, chiropractic, and massage therapy. I gained some improvement for a while. Then, in late 2001, the problem was getting more and more pronounced with frequent prescribed use of Milk of Magnesia; as well as frequent use of a warm water or saline enema to help start defecation; more and more pain in the upper right abdomen; and increasingly severe pain in the lower abdomen.

I lived with continuous back pain and back/abdominal spasms that would occasionally stop me in my tracks and almost trigger a fall. Movement (walking, sitting up and down, etc.) became hard or almost impossible without assistance for several days or weeks. Bed rest often was required. On occasion, when getting up and down or attempting to walk, I would have to use an aid (a cane, walking stick, walker, or another person's assistance) until the spasm/s abated. Sometimes it took hours, sometimes days, occasionally weeks, before my symptoms would improve.

I finally returned to Dr. A who again suggested a colectomy based on tests from years earlier. It was I who suggested that perhaps we repeat those tests or do other tests first. She said it wouldn't hurt to repeat the defagram and colonoscopy. The defagram (x-rays taken while the patient attempts to pass material through the rectum) showed a continuing rectocele (weakness of the rectum) and inadequate relaxation of the puborectalis muscle (spasm of the muscles surrounding the anus which do not allow adequate opening of the anus to permit passage of stool).

At that point, Dr. A wanted to send me for biofeedback at Hospital A. I thought the biofeedback technician was quite personable and concerned. But the biofeedback itself left a lot to be desired. I was told after the first most uncomfortable session to practice straining as though I was trying to have a bowel movement or pass gas. For two weeks I did so and during that time I realized I could not "feel" anything on my left side (the entire lower left quadrant of my abdomen).

At the second biofeedback session, while probes were in place (rectally), I was once more asked to strain repeatedly as if trying to have a bowel movement. Still, I could not "feel" that lower left side; clearly, it was numb. Within minutes after leaving the hospital that time I began having horrific rectal spasms. I refused to return for further biofeedback sessions and asked Dr. A for a referral to a physical therapist because "I could not feel anything on that left side." "Sure," she said, without questions, "if that's what you want," and she wrote a referral for physical therapy.

Also, about this time, Dr. A told me that I did not need a colectomy anyway, that I apparently had a muscle problem and we talked about my seeing some other doctor. We discussed the fact that there had been suggestions in the past about lupus being part of my overall health picture and she recommended Dr. E, a rheumatologist. So, I made appointments with Dr. E and Physical Therapist A.

I saw Physical Therapist A several times and regained what appeared to be normal bowel function for a while. It was amazing. For nearly three months I had bowel movements almost daily with only an occasional dose of Milk of Magnesia. I worked in my yard and garden and felt better than I had in a very long time.

Then one day, in early summer, I cleaned out my closet and had an asthma attack that night. My inhaler did not work well for that attack, so I also took a dose of oral medication (albuterol elixer) for the wheezing. Shortly thereafter my gut went into some kind of horrific spasm. My four-year-old granddaughter was spending the night with me and she observed the allergy and asthma attack, as well as the development of the abdominal spasm. It was a long night, in which she asked twice, "Grandma, WHY didn't you wear a mask when you cleaned out the dusty closet?" It is a question I still ask myself.

With the hideous abdominal pain and spasm apparently brought on again by the medication, the inability to defecate without major intervention returned. I asked for another referral for physical therapy. This time, therapy did not help. I have always felt and stated repeatedly that my use of bronchodilators for asthma/wheezing have played a role in the systemic spasms to which I am prone and have expressed this concern to all my doctors at one time or another.

Lesson Learned

When cleaning out a dusty closet, wear a good mask if you are allergic to dust!

Surgery Becomes Necessary

Bowel movements became more and more infrequent, and I began to feel really sick. Nausea and vomiting started. I lost weight and reached the point where I required Golight (a strong prescription laxative commonly used to cleanse the bowel prior to major diagnostic procedures) to have any bowel movement at all. This was the worst attack or bout I had ever had. I returned to Dr. A, and once more, she said the only thing she could offer me at that point was a colectomy since total colonic inertia had now occurred. Finally, I agreed for her to remove my colon.

We went to her conference room where we sat down to discuss my best options which she said was an iliostomy (an opening in the abdomen requiring that a bag be attached to the small bowel as it rests against the skin) in light of the problems I was having with inadequate relaxation of the puborectalis muscle, or a total colectomy with anastomosis (a direct connection with suture or titanium) of the small bowel to the rectum. My husband expressed concern at the iliostomy being an option before trying the anastomosis.

[NOTE: *When the intestines are removed, the body must have an alternate way for stool to leave the body, so the surgeon creates an opening in the abdomen for stool to pass through. The surgery to create the new opening is called ostomy. The opening is called a stoma to which a specially designed bag is attached to collect stool. The bag is emptied regularly throughout the day. Different types of ostomy are performed depending on how much and what part of the intestines are removed. The surgeries are called ileostomy and colostomy. When the colon and rectum are removed, the surgeon performs an ileostomy to attach the bottom of the small intestine (ileum) to the stoma. When only part of the colon or rectum is removed, the surgeon will perform a colostomy to attach the colon to the stoma.]*

I expressed my confidence that Dr. A would know what was required once she got inside my abdomen. I verbalized my concern about the recurrence of the rectocele or enterocele; specifically, I asked her if she could do the procedure by herself to repair and prevent future recurrence of these problems. Dr. C, my gynecologist, had expressed a willingness to assist with the surgery and see to such a repair himself if she needed him. She assured me she could handle it and did not need his help. Shortly before my scheduled surgery I saw Dr. C again and we discussed the upcoming surgery. I told him what Dr. A had said and he encouraged me, assuring me she would indeed do just what she had said she would do. He just cautioned me to remind her of my suture allergies.

[NOTE: An enterocele is a form of pelvic organ prolapse that occurs when the tissues and muscles that hold the small bowel in place become stretched or weakened. This weakening can cause the small bowel to move from its natural position and press into

the wall of the vagina. This slipping, falling down or
entrapment of the small bowel into abdominal space certainly
can limit motility of the bowel.]

Pre-op Maneuvers

On Thursday prior to surgery, I was due back at Dr.
A's office for what I had been told would be a history
and physical. Again, my husband went with me. I was
quite ill. Dr. A was more than an hour late coming in
that afternoon. She whizzed into the room with a
rapid apology for her tardiness to which I said, "no
problem, we don't mind" and she quickly reminded
me that I might not, but she had a whole waiting
room full of people who might.

She spent approximately (actually, a maximum of)
three minutes in the room, briefly listening to my
heart and lungs then quickly filled out a one-page
history and physical (H&P) sheet. She then walked
my husband and me to the checkout desk, gave the
H&P sheet to the receptionist there and told her to
attach my personal four-page history which I had
brought in that day to go over with her, and send me
for my blood work.

She told me she would see me on Monday. Then she
turned to a fellow physician who had just walked into
the office and began to excitedly discuss with him the

challenging surgery that had made her late coming in that afternoon. On that day, because she was so rushed and because I did not insist, as part of my history and physical visit, we, together, did not review again my past medical or allergy history. Clearly, this would prove to be a mistake as there are apparently some things that should be repeated over and over and over.

My husband and I were then directed to Hospital A for pre-op lab work. I left the paperwork with the staff in the lab where I was instructed to use the phone on the wall (in the lab) to schedule my nurse assessment for the following day. I dialed the number I had been given and the person who answered told me to call the hospital at 4:30 PM the next day for the nurse assessment.

Around 2:30 the following day, the nurse assessor called me and asked if it would be convenient for me if we did my assessment early since her schedule permitted. This nurse caller and I went over my four-page history in detail. When we hung up, she called back several times during the afternoon, once to ask if I was very sensitive to chemicals, as well as all the other things listed on my paperwork. Absolutely, I told her, numerous chemicals and fragrances. I was impressed with her repeated calls and her attention to detail. I felt cared for, and cared about, even safe.

Defining Months of 2002/2003...

Hospital A

On Monday, I was admitted to Hospital A for surgery.

My sister, Tamra, an operating room nurse, was with me and she carried two copies of my four-page medical history which included notes regarding allergies and sensitivities. We went over my history in detail with both the Pre-Op nurse, the anesthesiologist, and a circulating O.R. nurse, all of whom were very professional and seemed thorough.

I felt comfortable. I was asked if I wanted to see an ostomy nurse (one who specializes in the care of ileostomies and colostomies). I said, yes, because, in her office two weeks prior to my surgery, Dr. A had reminded me that my problems evacuating or passing bowel contents may not go away with an anastomosis, and she had recommended an iliostomy (a bag). After my husband had spoken up to ask if there was not something we could try first, she had said, yes, that she could go ahead and do the anastomosis, and if I "blew it," then she could do the iliostomy.

This had worried me because I knew my medical history and was so aware of how well I do NOT tolerate surgery. I had written a last-minute note to Dr. A regarding this concern, so I asked for the ostomy nurse consultation. Again, this nurse was extraordinarily professional. She answered my questions and marked my abdomen for a proper fit for the bag if indeed the surgeon chose to go with that procedure. Still, I was comfortable.

Then someone asked if they could rub my back and relax me. Sure, I said. Shortly after the back rub began, I started itching. I quickly discovered that my back was being rubbed with the contents of some kind of patient care packet that contained aloe, to which I am allergic. My sister and the nurse got cool wet clothes and tried to clean off my back.

The nurse would not give me any pre-op medication until I spoke to Dr. A regarding the possible ostomy and other issues that concerned me. When my doctor came in, I again mentioned my suture allergy and the issues I had written down.

The other things I mentioned to her and had put in a written memo were:

1 - If you know in your heart that I need, or eventually will need, a permanent iliostomy, I would much rather have it now than risk blowing the anastomosis and requiring a second surgery.

2 - I am very concerned about the area up under my diaphragm and around my liver where it frequently feels like there is a constricting band. I have been unable to wear a bra for two years because of this sometimes-extreme discomfort. Even when I do not feel a binding or constriction, I still have an uncomfortable fullness in the area.

3 - If you do go with the anastomosis, please do what you can to reinforce my pelvic floor support system. Besides the history of hysterectomy, cystocele, rectocele, and enterocele, I had 15 days of coughing in 1995 when I broke ribs (from continuous coughing — caused by my developing a horrific sensitivity to Sudafed which had never bothered before) and lost all bladder control, and my pelvic floor has never been the same. In recent months, the low backache has become as painful at times as it was before my hysterectomy.

Dr. A responded that she was not planning to be "in there" all afternoon and stuck the paper in her pocket. Then I went to surgery still itching from the back rub.

Lesson Learned

If your surgeon appears impatient with you PRIOR to surgery, I suggest that you consider canceling the surgery, if that is an option and find another surgeon. That impatience may be fleeting, or it may grow stronger and potentially more damaging after the procedure. In some areas, the surgeon may be the only specialist available; thus, he or she may feel they can behave anyway they like. Sadly, that may be true. When that is the case, often the hospital nursing staff may try to make up for some of the physician's rudeness. In the past, I have been in positions as a nurse to try to do that; I have even tried to defend or make excuses for such behavior. Certainly, the family or friend can stand near and help do damage control. Ideally, surgeons could attempt to view their patient as a whole person and try to be more sensitive. That, however, requires time. Time is money… so let's don't bet on that happening. Hope for it, but don't bet your life or the life on someone you love on it. There are physician healers and there are surgeons. When you discover a surgeon healer, then sing his or her praises from the roof tops. They deserve high praise and recognition. In fact, it would be awesome if they could be cloned! They, in my limited experience, appear to be a rare breed.

After Surgery

I was told that following the surgery Dr. A went out to speak to my family and friends. She related that she had removed the colon, was able to leave a short segment of the sigmoid (last section of the colon that leads to the rectum) and had done the anastomosis. In other words, she had cut out most of my colon and reattached what was left to the small bowel with titanium staples. She was very brief and a bit rude, according to family members who later told me that she had appeared impatient in response to their attempt to ask questions regarding the procedure. They said she assured them that I was "just fine," and she left the hospital.

Lesson Learned

Rudeness is never appropriate and cannot be therapeutic in a healthcare setting.

Nausea and itching were present when I awoke from surgery and continued once I was in my room which was very hot when I was taken into it from the recovery room. Maintenance was called and a large oscillating fan was brought to the room to be used until the air conditioning for that room could be repaired and working again.

This is when things begin to get fuzzy for me... The first 48 hours in that room are not clear in my memory. Beyond that period, I do know that some degree of nausea was ever present. I remember rude nursing/auxiliary staff. I recall repeated and violent projectile vomiting episodes (projectile means the vomitus would shoot out with force and land several feet from my body!). I vividly recall that my sister/s and friends administered most of my personal care (bathing me or assisting with my bath, measuring intake and output, cleaning up when I would vomit, etc.) because the staff (most of them, especially the nursing assistants) wore such strong fragrances. When they would enter the room I would feel, not only nausea, but it would feel like my stomach would jump or lurch, which under the circumstances was extraordinarily painful.

Within minutes after the antagonizing smell was gone the stomach pain would calm down, usually without medication, but the nausea took longer to abate, and it never totally went away. As I recall, I only asked for pain medication when pain in my upper right abdomen would be really bad. Also, I noticed that the shots for nausea never totally stopped the nausea that would be made worse every time I got a whiff of the fragrances from the hall.

I had frequently had such stomach lurching, vomiting episodes over the years when I would be subjected to certain odors, primarily chemicals and petroleum products. Perfumed fragrances had never caused such violent reaction, but I assumed that was what was going on for the first few days. It never occurred to me that I had an ileus (air trapped in my small bowel) that might have been a serious precipitating factor. Not even when I asked for x-rays, or tests, or "something…" to help determine why I still felt so sick by the end of the week did I have a clue what was so wrong. I just knew something was not right.

Dear Doctor, I am your teacher…

Lesson Learned

It can be potentially dangerous, even life-threatening for patient, or doctor, to just assume anything.

Know this:
EFFECTIVE COMMUNICATION
ALWAYS REQUIRES ADEQUATE RESPONSE.

The room air conditioning was repaired by the end of my first day of hospitalization, but, all week, we requested that the fan remain in my room. We kept it turned toward the door to help blow odors/fragrances out and away from me. My family and friends would stop everyone at the door and check them for fragrance before allowing them to enter. Several staff members were very rude when confronted about this.

On one occasion, my sister literally blocked the door and would not allow one nursing assistant to enter the room because of her very strong perfume. My sister went to a head nurse and discussed the attitude/behavior of staff. The nurse she addressed said that she had trouble believing that anybody could be so allergic or sensitive as I claimed to be, as evidenced in my personal four-page history from my home computer that we had requested be part of the chart.

The nurse said none of my allergies/sensitivities were "in the system" but my sister pointed out that my history (the four pages) was indeed in the chart. My sister told the nurse on duty that she too was a nurse, and she knew how hard it was to believe some things that were on /in patient histories/charts, but that whether any nurse believed it, did not matter. She told her the fact is that the patient's account of his or her medical history is part of the medical record, and the nurse must respect it and act accordingly.

Lesson Learned

Perhaps, family and friends who sit with hospital patients should limit the personal care services they give. My family and I should have adamantly insisted on nursing care being administered by fragrance free staff. A verbal report of vomiting or other issues may not linger long in the mind of the one to whom it is reported. However, when that staff member actually cleans up the mess, they will be more likely to remember to chart it.

In my case, the history was gone over very well on the Friday before my admission, by what had appeared to be a very detailed oriented telephone nurse, yet the floor duty nurse claimed that no notes had made it "into the system" regarding any allergies, sensitivities, or special needs. Even though we had brought in another copy of my medical history on the morning of surgery and had gone over it in detail with pre-op personnel, the floor staff may not have been accustomed to looking for such hard copy paperwork. We wrongly assumed that all healthcare professionals involved in my care knew about my history and special needs. Not until this communication occurred between my sister and the nurse on the floor was any effort made to bring attention to the allergies and special needs. By then, I had already been "labeled" a troublesome patient, at best.

Lesson Learned

Never assume (especially in this electronic era) that any health care provider is aware of a patient's medical history just because the patient or some family member might have shared it verbally or even submitted it in writing to be part of the patient's past or present chart or records. I repeat: Never assume anything. Be certain of the facts whenever possible. Also, know that technological dependence can serve well those who depend on it only if timely and accurate data has been put into an electronic system. Remember, those who input such data are human and humans err, so check and recheck the facts.

Help Comes

At one point, a nursing assistant was pulled from another floor to help my sister with my care. The mess I had made was too much for my sister to clean up alone. I recall well my conversation with this person. She was very apologetic and compassionate. She told me she had been pulled to that same floor on which I was a patient on previous occasions for the exact same reason. She said she herself had chronic sinus problems and had repeatedly complained to management about the fragrances, but to no avail. She encouraged me to address the issue with management because she had personal hopes that management would eventually listen to a patient; thus her own situation might improve. I assured her that I would address the issue when I was well enough to come back and do so. She said that would be wonderful because she had spent 15 years at that job and could not afford to quit. She repeatedly stressed how much she understood what I was going through because of how her own health had been affected by the fragrances.

I recall how every time my food tray came to my room that it had products on it to which I was allergic. After speaking with the nurses regarding dietary needs, still nothing came from the dietary department that I could tolerate. My family brought in canned broth and bottled water from outside one of the most prominent and highly rated hospitals in the city. On the last day that I was at the hospital, a dietician came to see me and said her department had only been notified that very day of my special dietary needs. She apologized for the "error."

I recall itching off and on, and occasionally feeling tightness in my chest, having headaches come and go, and just generally feeling really bad. The nurses kept asking about my pain, but I did not consider the pain a big deal – it was not much worse than what I had experienced for months prior to surgery, except during the vomiting episodes. Most of the pain was in the upper right quadrant of my abdomen and I asked Dr. A about it. She said that was because "she had taken down a lot of adhesions in that area."

I believe she did that, but I never found evidence or documentation of this in any of the operative records that I later obtained. I continue to have pain in this area, front and back. Spasm-like discomfort occasionally will spread all over the abdomen especially across the diaphragm – often like a constricting band. Still, I seldom wear a bra because of this ongoing issue.

My surgery was on a Monday. By Saturday I was really feeling "sick" – very weak, nauseous and a different "sick" from what I had known earlier. The weakness was so profound that I had concerns about my thyroid function/maintenance being really out of kilter. A duty nurse assured me that could not be the case, and that I easily could go a month without my Synthroid (thyroid medication), without incurring a problem. I told her that she was wrong, that I personally could not do that without getting into trouble, that my thyroid levels had always been hard to maintain, and that other physicians had cautioned me about this. I insisted that Dr. A be notified.

I became convinced that my electrolytes must be very out of balance and that I was experiencing hypothyroid symptoms as well. I thought I might be having medication absorption issues, with vomiting having occurred on numerous occasions during the month prior to my surgery, and during which time I had lost several pounds. I wanted blood work done. I asked for it. It did not happen. I also thought an x-ray of my abdomen would have been ordered at some point, considering the projectile vomiting that I was having off and on, and I expressed my concern. The nurse tried to call Dr. A, but said she only was able to contact another physician, whom I had never heard of and who was not part of Dr. A's physician practice group. He was covering for Dr. A, and though the nurse said he was "in the hall just around the corner," she said he refused to come to my room and see me.

On Saturday night, following surgery on Monday, I was at my lowest point with rude nurses/nursing assistants, and little or no "doctoring" to say the least.

On two occasions Dr. A only came to the door to my room and did not enter all the way since she, too, was wearing fragrance. Yet, I saw later in my medical records where she had – apparently out of habit or as was her charting routine – made notes every day that my "abdomen was soft and chest clear." My constant companions – I literally was never left alone – are witnesses to the fact that, on two occasions, Dr. A only made comments from a distance and did not approach my bed. Thus, the charted information was inappropriate.

Very late on Saturday night, as I continued to feel sicker and sicker, I asked for a chaplain. The chaplain came to me promptly. She was a lovely African American. She was so beautiful and was wearing no fragrance and she prayed louder than anybody I had ever heard pray! She touched me. She held my hand. She patted my arm. Compassion oozed from her. It was a first for the week from anybody on staff at that hospital!

Even the staff who did present themselves somewhat professionally, did not do so warmly. I remember praying silently that night that I could just live… and I asked God for the courage and guidance to somehow, at some future time, be able to address the importance of competent and compassionate behavior in such settings.

Lesson Learned

Teaching competent compassionate behavior to employees may be a good idea in all businesses; requiring such behavior is necessary in the health professions. There should be more and better education for patients and the health care professionals who care for them. Common sense should rule, and compassionate competence should be two everyday buzz words in hospitals and health care settings everywhere.

The next morning when Dr. A came, and actually entered into the room, I told her I was sick and felt like I needed blood work and other tests. That is when she told me she was the doctor, and I was the patient and that I did not need to tell her what I thought she should do – that I just needed to tell her how I felt.

I started crying softly and all I could say was "I feel sick." I remember feeling disgusted by the weak whimpering sound of my voice. I had no fight left in me. I felt horribly defeated. It did not seem to matter that the projectile vomiting was continuing. It did not matter that I repeatedly had told Dr. A, and the nursing staff, how the various smells were making my stomach do flips. I felt cold, and the cramping feeling in my abdomen would not get better; in fact, it seemed to be getting worse. Low grade fever continued, but nobody there thought my elevated temperature was of any concern. I just felt like I was getting sicker, not better, and I had said so over and over to no avail.

And so... once I said, "I feel sick" one last time, I hushed. I lay there quietly fighting tears and longing for all 5'8" of me to curl up into a little ball and vanish. I had never felt so small. I desperately wanted to disappear. Clearly, I was not important; and my complaints, along with a week's worth of requests for help were not important. I did not matter.

Dr. A told me that "any blood work would not be normal because I had just had major surgery, and there was no need to do it anyway." She then told me the best thing to do was get me out of the hospital as soon as possible. That is when my sister offered to take me out then and there. Dr. A said we should wait until the next day. She clearly indicated that I was just a problem patient who could not be satisfied while in the hospital. Getting me out of the hospital as soon as possible was her only answer. She was extremely rude, appeared angry, and emphatically told me I was just like every nurse-patient she had ever had and that nurses were the worst patients.

That Sunday, the seventh day following the surgery, Lynda (my sister) somehow managed to get someone to clean my room for the first time since I had been admitted seven days earlier. Hospital personnel repeatedly had said they could not clean my room because they had nothing to use that was fragrance free. My sister finally and forcefully suggested plain water and a clean mop. The room was very dusty, and my sister thought because of my allergies that the dust might be a factor in making me feel so bad.

…I cannot really describe how I felt after that Sunday visit by Dr. A. I know I was much more upset, and I was briefly tearful. My sister tried to soothe me by reassuring me that I would leave the hospital the next day, pointing out how maybe the dirty room and the fragrances were at the root of my problems, and, hopefully, I would feel better at home. But the low-grade fever remained, and I continued to feel very weak and oh, how my abdomen cramped. The nausea and vomiting would not let up. I began to feel like I was just being a baby – a real wimp. A friend, Peggy, came up on Sunday afternoon to spend the evening and night with me.

On the day that I left the hospital, the charge nurse came in to remove the staples from my incision and while she was doing it (ungloved) her cell phone rang and she reached into her pocket, took it out and talked, put it back into her pocket then resumed removal of my staples. In time, I would learn that she did not get all the staples. Another surgeon would later remove the remainders.

Lesson Learned

Common sense is not common anymore. At this writing, in 2005, recent studies have revealed that TV Remote controls in patient's hospital rooms have been discovered to be major germ spreading vehicles. So, well, yeah…. I can only imagine how many germs are on the telephones that hospital staff carry with them from room to room!

I do not think I ever have been anywhere in my life where I felt like folks wanted me gone as strongly as the staff at Hospital A seemed to want me gone. It was on my last day there that the dietician came by to apologize for the lack of attention to my dietary restrictions, saying she had just been notified that very day of my allergies, sensitivities, and special needs. When I was absolutely ready to leave – I mean within minutes of leaving the hospital that I wanted to be gone from as much as or more than the staff wanted me gone – while the wheelchair was being retrieved, I asked once more to speak to the nurse manager in charge of the floor I was on. This time, I was told she would come to my room.

I then hurriedly scribbled notes. If I was going to be heard, in the few minutes I had left in that facility, I wanted to be able to say it all – to hold nothing back now that I was leaving. The people I was about to report could no longer hurt me. Yes, absolutely, I had started to feel paranoid, and for good reason. Earlier calls to complain had brought no results, but this time someone really came to my room. Upon her arrival, I very emotionally blurted out how rudely I had been treated. I told of how nurses and nursing assistants had literally laughed and made fun of my complaints about the extreme sensitivity to fragrances, dust, and mold.

"All I have on is a little cologne (or body wash, or

hair gel…) but okay, I won't come in if you don't want me to" was what we would hear repeatedly, shift after shift, day after day. At other times, people who smelled strongly literally tried to push themselves into the room – thus leading, on one occasion, to a near confrontation between my sister and one nursing assistant. I told her how I had vomited and vomited and that it was my sisters who had to clean me up every time. It was family who had tried to keep my room clean and wiped down for dust as best they could. I told her how one sister had finally demanded the room be mopped on my seventh day there and how personnel repeatedly, and on occasion, somewhat haughtily, had said they could not do it because they had nothing to use that was "fragrance free."

I told her of the air conditioning problem on the first day and how hot and nauseous I had been. I told her how the TV had come on and off at will (which was no big deal except it would wake me if I happened to be asleep, and sleep was so precious). I described how the shower chair was dangerously wobbly and had tilted over with me twice. I told her that the only chair in the room – the one that was right beside my bed – had dust and mildew in and under the torn cushion. We had asked for another chair and the response from personnel who overheard our request was "What do they want now? Do they need a special chair too?" Our request was denied. We were told there were no more chairs. My sister, who cared for me for five days and nights, had to sit up around the clock in that one chair. She chose not to recline it at night for fear of further releasing mold spores or dust into the air. Absolutely no one offered to help make her more comfortable.

With tears of release streaming down my cheeks, I told of how the maintenance man had once come barreling – directly behind his loud knock without even waiting for a response – into the room with a ladder and tools. The companion sitting with me promptly made him turn around. He protested that he needed to drill a hole in the sheetrock and put up some boxes or shelving. She told him he would have to do it later. He protested – demanding to know why. She told him that I was sick and highly allergic and that he could not come in to work and cut sheetrock while I was in that room. Here again there were sneers and giggles from the hall as he retreated, and the distinct comment from one nursing assistant was, "I see they won't let you in either – they have to smell of us before we can go in," followed by snickering.

I told her of how I had waited one time for an hour and a half for a blown IV to be removed from a swelling arm. The IV team nurse who finally came to remove it apologized sincerely. She said she had "just been told" and came promptly upon being told she was needed. She apologized repeatedly. I believed her and felt that the floor staff had deliberately ignored me or put me off. I felt it was their way of punishing me for being a bad patient.

I told her that a lot of people might have done a lot of things right for a long time for this particular hospital to somehow have held on to its "center of excellence" claim, but there had been no indication during my stay that there was any truth to the claim, and that, as far as I was concerned, this hospital had long outlived any such ranking.

Lesson Learned

A Patient's Bill of Rights should be posted in every healthcare facility, and it should mean something to all hospital employees. They should be required to memorize it before being hired and recite it anew before receiving salary increases. If Hospital A's own well publicized version of its Patient's Bill of Rights had simply been honored as they were given to me in August 2002 in my "Welcome" packet, I can only imagine how different the weeks, months and years following my surgery could have been.

NOTE: *A Patient's Bill of Rights was adopted by the US Advisory Commission on Consumer Protection and Quality in the Health Care Industry in 1998. Many health plans, organizations and facilities have adopted the principles. The American Hospital Association (www.aha.org) offered a Patient's Bill of Rights in 1973, then revised it in 1992 to a much more detailed and generic explanation brochure fully explaining the rights and responsibilities of patients. Various healthcare organizations and some states have officially adopted a Patient's Bill of Rights which is prominently posted in hospitals and other facilities. The Patient's Bill of Rights as adopted in 1998, and posted at www.cancer.org as of 12-1-05, consisted primarily of the following (I cannot find this list of "rights" anywhere now, as of August 2021):*

Information Disclosure.
You have the right to accurate and easily understood information about your health plan, health care professionals, and health care facilities. If you speak another language, have a physical or mental disability, or just don't understand something, assistance will be provided so you can make informed health care decisions.

Choice of Providers and Plans.
You have the right to a choice of health care providers that is sufficient to provide you with access to appropriate high-quality health care.

Access to Emergency Services.
If you have severe pain, an injury, or sudden illness that convinces you that your health is in serious jeopardy, you have

the right to receive screening and stabilization emergency services whenever and wherever needed, without prior authorization or financial penalty.

Participation in Treatment Decisions.
You have the right to know your treatment options and to participate in decisions about your care. Parents, guardians, family members, or other individuals that you designate can represent you if you cannot make your own decisions.

Respect and Nondiscrimination.
You have a right to considerate, respectful, and nondiscriminatory care from your doctors, health plan representatives, and other health care providers.

Confidentiality of Health Information.
You have the right to talk in confidence with health care providers and to have your health care information protected. You also have the right to review and copy your own medical record and request that your physician change your record if it is not accurate, relevant, or complete.

Complaints and Appeals.
You have the right to a fair, fast, and objective review of any complaint you have against your health plan, doctors, hospitals, or other health care personnel. This includes complaints about waiting times, operating hours, the conduct of health care personnel, and the adequacy of health care facilities.

In 2003, the AHA updated the Bill of Rights
again and renamed it "The Patient Care
Partnership." Then, on June 22, 2010,
President Obama announced new interim
final regulations, the Patient's Bill of Rights,
that included a set of protections that apply to
health coverage starting on or after
September 23, 2010, six months after the
enactment of the Affordable Care Act.

Today, at this final editing of this manuscript, in 2021,
at the American Hospital Association website there is
a downloadable brochure that is designed with these
headings:

The Patient Care Partnership
Understanding Expectations, Rights and Responsibilities
What to expect during your hospital stay:
- High quality hospital care
- A clean and safe environment
- Involvement in your care
- Protection of your privacy
- Preparing you and your family when you leave the
hospital
- Help with your bill and filing insurance claims

I strongly suggest you study that brochure and focus
on the word "partnership."
It's your body.

In looking back, I have no idea where or how I came up with the strength or courage at that point to make my grievances known to that nurse manager. I do know, absolutely, that I am a born and bred patient advocate, ever the one to stand up for others in need. In fact, such a trait has landed me in more than one precarious position over the years. We often can fight for others when we will not or cannot any longer fight for ourselves. I suspect it was partially for the benefit of others who would follow after me that I made that last effort to be heard.

I remember how the nurse manager started to cry right along with me. When I had finished talking, she tearfully apologized profusely, and added, "I knew we had been having problems, but I thought things had gotten better."

Just prior to my dismissal, blood was drawn for a CBC. Routine, I was told. Just a CBC, no other blood work, and, still, there was no interest in doing an x-ray or any other studies. Everything I was going through was "normal post-op" according to the doctor and staff. I left the hospital with my temperature still close to 100 degrees. I was wheeled out to go home wearing double surgical masks to help diminish the effects of traffic fumes, as well as other odors and smells while enroute to my home to which I so very much longed to return.

Lesson Learned

Worth pointing out at this point is how in the early years of managed care, some contracts between doctors and insurance companies were set up in such a way that the doctor stood to make more money for doing less. The more money the doctor saved the insurance company, by not ordering too many procedures or tests, then the better the bottom line was for the doctor at the month's or year's end. I do not know if such year-end bonuses are still offered or not, and I have no way of knowing if that may have been a factor in my own case. I do know that patients would be wise to ask about this type of potential doctor and insurance company policy or agreement before putting their lives into the hands of a physician whose bottom line could potentially mean more to him or her than the patient means.

I was weaker still, and thoroughly exhausted by the time I got home that Monday afternoon, and even more nauseous. By the time I arrived, the vomiting had started again. Even tiny sips of liquids like apple juice, potato soup, and Gatorade would seem to actually stimulate me to throw up. With any attempt to take in fluids I always vomited. Occasionally it would be a projectile action, just like at the hospital. The diarrhea, as well, which I believed to be normal in my new post-op state, continued. My husband and sister-in-law were constantly with me, and they took turns supporting me while I would vomit. Repeatedly, I accommodated the basin they so readily and lovingly provided. By bedtime on Monday, just six hours after returning home, I was too weak to sit up without assistance.

I have been unable to find any reference made in my hospital chart regarding the projectile vomiting. (I requested a copy of the records a couple of months after the surgery, and after I paid a very nice fee for them, they were mailed to me in total disarray. In fact, they were in a most haphazard disorder.) I know that at least one nurse had witnessed the projectile vomiting and she even asked how often I had been vomiting like that, because I barely missed her, while spraying my sister instead, who was standing at the foot of the bed. My family and I repeatedly reported the force with which I vomited at times. I was repeatedly informed that what I was going through was normal or "expected under the circumstances." I did not believe that then. I do not believe it now.

The next day (Tuesday AM) we called Dr. A's office and asked the receptionist/nurse to have the doctor call me. The person on the phone asked what the problem was. We told her that I could not stop vomiting. We also asked for the report on my bloodwork. She called back a couple of hours later (Dr. A never called me) and told me that Dr. A said the nausea was never going away until I started eating. She said Dr. A said to tell me that I was a nurse, and I should know that I was going to have to start eating before I would get better. She told me that Dr. A said to forget all previous dietary guidelines (a copy of which I had never actually been given – nor had I received any verbal instructions) and to eat anything I wanted.

I asked my sister-in-law to prepare oatmeal since it was one of the first things I had been served at the hospital. I ate small amounts but could not retain it. The nausea and smell and hideously rotten taste inside of me was becoming more and more unbearable. (I later was told by the dietician at Hospital B that oatmeal should not have been part of my diet for weeks or maybe even months after the surgery I'd just had.)

On the next day, I continued to grow weaker. We called my new Primary Care Provider's (PCP's) office to find out if he could send a home healthcare nurse to evaluate my condition and do some blood work.

He said that I would have to call Dr. A's office yet again for that order since he knew nothing about what had gone on over the past ten days. We called Dr. A's office once more and made that request. We waited throughout the day for a home healthcare nurse to show up. A friend and neighbor (a Registered Nurse) who lived just up the road came over in the late afternoon at my husband's request. She immediately told my husband to load me in the car and get me to a hospital STAT (immediately!).

Hospital B – trip one

I was admitted with dehydration, electrolytes considerably out of balance, an ileus with partial small bowel blockage, an abdominal abscess, and still just low grade fever, though the white blood cell count was starting to climb at that point. I had repeatedly told deaf ears that I did not experience high fevers – that 99-100 degrees meant something was wrong with my body. Many years prior, the thoracic surgeon I spoke of earlier had cautioned me not to ever use my temperature as a guide. "Always listen to your body," he had stressed. Sadly, all the listening I had done over the past ten days had done nothing for me, since those I looked to for help did not listen to me.

At Hospital B, both the ER physician, Dr. F, and the gastroenterologist who was called in, Dr. G, had been advised of the events of the past week and made aware of how I felt about my recent experience in the previous hospital. Yet they persuaded me to let them call in Dr. H, a surgeon in the same large physician group with Dr. A. They said they felt like I may have to be taken back to surgery, that they were between a rock and hard place, and that he was all they had. They assured me that he was conscientious and could do well any work required of him. The coming weeks and months would prove they were so right!

Hospital B emergency room personnel and every nurse and doctor in the entire building were unbelievable (truly unbelievable at this point!). They were compassionate and competent, and NOBODY was wearing any fragrance. I was assured that Hospital B was a fragrance-free facility and that I would not have a fragrance problem there. I WAS SO THANKFUL.

Lesson Learned

Somebody should see to it that every hospital or skilled nursing facility is fragrance free. "Do not wear fragrance and do not wear jewelry when giving patient care" was one of the first things I was taught in nursing school. I am under the impression that it is still taught. It does not take someone who is extra sensitive like I am to react to fragrances or odors of any kind in a hospital. I am told that the number of hyper-sensitive patients is rapidly climbing because autoimmune disease is on the rise. Whether they are hyper or hypo sensitive, or somewhere in between, most patients are sick when they go to hospitals. All patients should have the right to expect to feel better and to get better, not worse! Fragrance free hospitals should be an absolute standard.

Within 24 hours, the abscess had been drained by Radiologist, Dr. J, in a well-prepared latex-free surgical setting where CAT scan equipment was used to assist with accurate aspiration technique. It was Dr. J's third day on staff and such CAT scan guided procedures were his specialty.

Antibiotics were started along with intravenous (IV) fluids and electrolyte replacement. Soon, for the first time since my surgery ten days earlier, I was beginning to feel safe and well cared for medically, but still extremely weak. A family member or a friend remained beside me at all times. I appreciated this tremendously. AND, Hospital B treated them royally, thanking them repeatedly for being there and seeking in every way to make them comfortable.

Nurses were constantly in and out of my room and if I had not observed the difference in the two facilities (Hospital A vs. Hospital B), I never would have believed such a contrast could exist! As matter of fact, in the Welcome Kit given to my family when I was admitted to Hospital B, family members were encouraged to stay with patients and recognized as a valuable member of the patient care team!

I was still very sick, but, oh so very thankful, to be receiving compassionate and competent medical attention. I recall Dr. K, the senior partner of the surgery group coming to visit me at Hospital B. He told me he had insisted that Dr. H take the day off.

(That is just how truly attentive and dedicated Dr. H was. Clearly, he wanted to keep a close watch over me. He was amazing!)

At first, I would not let Dr. K touch me and I resented his being there, though he eventually came across as decent enough, concerned, willing to listen, and knowledgeable. He let me talk; actually, he strongly encouraged me to vent. I remember wondering, at one point, if he really was concerned about me, or if he just wanted to try to discern how much trouble his partner might be in. He was smooth, but I will give him the benefit of the doubt and believe it was both. He offered to go with me to meet with administration officials at Hospital A if I decided to make formal complaints about my stay there. (That's what I mean about "smooth.")

I told him I expected him to discipline both Dr. A, and Dr. L. Of course, I never knew who Dr. L was or how he came to be covering for Dr. A on that Saturday when the nurse said that she made repeated calls to ask a physician to come by and talk to me about any potential bloodwork or tests that could be done to uncover why I felt so bad. The nurse told me that Dr. L did tell her that she could give me another IV, in case it was a low potassium issue. Later, I observed Dr. K's name in my Hospital A records, but I never saw him while I was there. I wondered if things would have been different if I had. Still later, I also wondered if he might have been the physician I would hear about who had gone to bat for the other special needs patient I would soon learn about who had received such excellent care following the same type surgery I'd had, on the same floor, at Hospital A.

Hospital B – trip two

At Hospital B, I soon started to show signs of improvement and was allowed to go back home after one week, but the very next day I was readmitted to Hospital B by ambulance. The ride home on the previous day had physically drained me and I'd had diarrhea again all night. Once more, I was dehydrated and experiencing low grade fever. By the time I reached the hospital I was vomiting again and had no control over my bladder or bowels. My electrolytes once more had dropped dramatically. I was so physically weak, and once again emotionally depleted. I prayed for death, in the back of the ambulance that day, though I never said so. Yet, it was as though the paramedic enroute, the nursing staff on arrival at the hospital, and even the ER doctor (the same Dr. F from the week before) seemed to understand.

Remarkably, the paramedic addressed the issue of my non verbalized desire to die head on. That is how strongly she seemed to sense my unexpressed thoughts. I remember being scared because I could no longer feel parts of my body. I literally had lost all feeling in both my legs. The weakness I was experiencing was profound and I felt like I was caught up in some zone where the choice really was mine: to live or to die. The paramedic asked if she could get a family member on her personal cell phone to talk to me. She called my son. He talked… I listened. Still, it was hard to choose life.

Within moments after I was readmitted through Hospital B's emergency room, Dr. F came over to me, bent down over the stretcher and whispered, "Mary Jane, I know you don't feel good. I know you feel really bad about yourself right now, but you are going to survive this. We are going to get you through it. You are going to feel better soon."

Crying, vomiting, urinating and defecating… while literally and uncontrollably expelling bodily fluids from just about every orifice and still unable to feel my legs, once more I reluctantly chose life. I also chose to trust these Hospital B doctors again. That ER physician, and numerous other specialists, would prove worthy of my trust.

All the ER and ICU staff who were assisting at this second visit to Hospital B, one right after the other, were constantly reassuring me while they attended to my escalating needs, did blood work, got IV's going again and called in the GI docs once more. Their attention, warmth and continuous words of encouragement were better than textbook perfection! By the time Dr. M, who was one of Dr. G's partners, showed up to do a history and officially admit me again, I was in a room and resting better, with IV's continuously going once more. And, finally, I could feel my legs. Both Dr. M and Dr. N, another of Dr. G's partners who was involved at this point, were extraordinarily nice. Warm. Professional. Thorough. Dr. M said he would call Dr. H and advise him that I had been readmitted and get him back on my case as well.

During this second stay at Hospital B, my asthma flared. I recall continued weakness and low-grade fever. I also recall that the doctors were not agreeing about how to treat me. I finally, at the end of another week of hospitalization, told them I wanted to go back home again. I also told Dr. H that, if I had to come back, I would only have him as the admitting or lead physician because he and I had developed a comfortable rapport. We all were puzzled about my symptoms, but I agreed more and more with Dr. H's line of thought and felt he was somehow more tuned in to what my body was doing than the GI guys were. Despite of his professional alliance with Dr. A, I really liked him and had grown to fully trust him.

Prior to requesting that I be allowed to go back home, I recall asking to see the notes my family had been jotting down. I read over them and looked over all my hospital medications. Although I still did not feel well, and one of the doctors – I do not recall which one – had even thrown out the suggestion that we might at some point need to rule out pericarditis (inflammation of the thin sac or pericardium that holds the heart) because of the profound weakness and continuing low grade fevers, I very much wanted to go home. Dr. H agreed to my terms – which were for me to go back on the home medications (different brands from what the hospital used) that I had been on prior to my surgery and discontinue the ones that I was being given at the hospital.

I personally felt that I was in a state of general inflammation, not true infection, but I still was instructed to continue the antibiotics for several weeks. Dr. H urged me to follow up with Dr. B, my Primary Care Provider, within the next day or two. He seemed to agree that it might be very beneficial for me to try to return to what I called my "normal environment and medication schedule."

It is worth noting here, for anyone else who might have problems tolerating pain management medications, as well as for those who would prefer not to take such systemic medications, that physical therapy modalities played a huge role in my ability to cope with the physical pain that accompanied this very trying time. Physical Therapist A, as well as Physical Therapist B who so capably had followed me for years, actually came to Hospital B and assisted me. They did this out of genuine compassion and concern. For months, Physical Therapist B followed up regularly. I always will be grateful for such attention that was beyond the call of duty and compensation.

Finding me again

Vindication teases me

I went home and followed up immediately with primary care provider, Dr. B. I took with me a list of discussion points and requests which he eagerly went over with me in detail. He ordered bloodwork, to recheck my potassium, calcium and my thyroid levels, a Complete Blood Count (CBC), liver profile, etc. He was very concerned.

I do not recall mentioning to the doctors at Hospital B that my thyroid function needed to be very closely watched. Actually, I don't recall trying to tell anybody at Hospital B what to do or how to do it. Only later would I come to realize that I actually had never tried to do that at Hospital A, either. All I had done was beg for help and ask that they do x-rays or blood tests or something. Anything. I was just thankful to be more cared for and "feel" safer and more cared about. I also was thankful when Dr. B's office nurse called to tell me that my potassium level was still low and my Thyroid Stimulating Hormone (TSH) was extremely elevated (indicating that I had not been absorbing my daily thyroid medication well enough to keep my thyroid function within normal range). Dr. B increased my thyroid medication (Synthroid) dosage and closely followed my blood levels for several months. If I had not still been so sick, I may have felt vindicated. Instead, I just continued to feel beat down emotionally and physically. Not only had I developed a partial blockage in my small intestine and an abscess, my electrolyte levels had been crazy for several weeks, and, just as I had suggested very early on at Hospital A, my thyroid function probably had been a major player all along in causing me to feel so bad.

Revelations come

As days passed, I also began to feel that I must be allergic to silk suture since I continued to feel so very inflamed internally. The burning, itching discomfort ruled my days and nights. I did not know that Dr. A's post-op dictation would later reveal to me that she had used Novofil suture (which I was told is the same as another brand of suture for which Dr. C had tested me and found me allergic.) There also would be a question that never goes away about Dr. A actually using Vicryl as well, to which I am very allergic. Her notes were contradictory in that she dictated that she used Vicryl in several places, but at the end of her typed dictation, she said no that she did not actually use the Vicryl, that she used silk instead "since the patient claimed to be allergic to Vicryl." Yet, follow up investigation would reveal that the hospital had billed me, not for just one, but for two packs of Vicryl. If, and this is a huge IF I am using: if the doctor and the operating room staff actually used all the correct suture material that my allergy history required, it could be that routine or habitual hospital billing procedures simply indicated otherwise. Because of all this confusion I truly cannot know what caused such an extended period of inflammation. Months later, when my PCP introduced steroids into my medication regimen, the inflammatory symptoms finally began to show some degree of improvement.

Lesson Learned

Though routines or standard operating procedures are time and cost saving measures that are used by every business, they can be dangerous not only to a person's health, but to bottom lines everywhere. When an occasional mistake or inaccuracy occurs, it may still be more cost effective to just pay for that one mistake than to require more detailed awareness on the part of all individuals involved in the care of patients, (or the building of an aircraft engine, the landing of an impaired jetliner, the manufacture of an automobile tire, the writing of an automobile maintenance procedure book…) Sometimes, standard operating procedures should NOT be the order of the day.

Perhaps, through routine or habit, Dr. A had misrepresented her medical services, or lack thereof, in her chart notes, as well, regarding daily examination of my chest and abdomen, since on two occasions she came no further than the door and once just to the end of my bed because she herself wore such strong fragrance. For all I knew, she had misrepresented herself in her dictation regarding the Vicryl. Habits are, after all, habits. All this… while we had told everybody in Pre-Op (the pre-surgery department) about the suture allergy, and the very last thing my sister said to operating room staff as I was wheeled away from her, was "check her suture allergies." Since this issue had been repeatedly discussed with the preadmission nurse who had called me on Friday before the surgery on Monday, there should have been no Vicryl or PDS or Novofil anywhere near me in that operating room! Perhaps it was Dr. A's habit to use Vicryl and so she used it, or maybe it was her habit to dictate that she used it and she just began her dictation that way and really did not use it. I will never know for sure what was or was not used.

Lesson Learned

When something is important, communicate the importance repeatedly to everyone involved and always in a timely manner. Some things cannot be repeated often enough.

Shame sets in

Another sister, and two sisters-in-law, took turns
staying with me at home for several weeks after that
final hospital dismissal near the end of August.
September was very emotional for me. I remember
feeling angry at Dr. A, and Hospital A. I also felt
guilty because I had wanted to die. I felt like a coward
– a baby, a real wimp. And I could not talk about my
experiences without trembling and having hard chills.
It was, in fact, very hard to talk at all. I felt so
ashamed. In my mind, I still was, after all, a "horrible
patient."

The worst yet...

Late September, and part of October, turned out to
be the worst yet. Something inside me, inside the
heart, soul, brain, and real essence of who I am,
simply turned off for a few weeks. I felt nothing. No
anger. No pain. No emotion at all – a first for me,
ever in my whole life. I felt like I was – in very slow
motion – going through only the minimally essential
motions of living. Neither thoughts of my
grandchildren nor visits from them could stir
anything within me. If that's depression, I can
understand how some people would end their lives.
There was just nothing. I had no enthusiasm, no
passion, or no feelings about family, friends or

anything else. Emotionally, there suddenly was absolutely nothing. I felt totally depleted of everything that made me who I had been.

Yet my family and friends kept calling and coming. Their support remained invaluable. I do not know how people survive without good support systems. Friends and family members would call daily to tell me how much they and God loved me and that they were praying for me. Near the end of my fourth week in this hideous empty grey/black state of being, I verbally released into the telephone a mouthful of horrific expletives at my sister and her God. To this day, it is still very hard for me to believe that I said what I said. I try hard not to replay it and would like to forget the moment.

It actually was not until later that afternoon that I myself heard what I had said. It happened while gazing out my back door at a beautiful old tree in the edge of the woods, trying hard to focus on the wooden swing that hung from one of its limbs – wanting to remember how I had loved that swing, and that tree, and those woods – and not understanding how I could still be alive to some degree, and functioning to some extent, yet feel so void of emotion. Suddenly, the morning's conversation started to replay itself inside my soul in a strange and slow kind of mental or emotional or spiritual motion. Somehow, something started to turn back on within me. As it did so, I cringed to hear myself replaying the words I had spoken a few hours earlier as I had described what I thought of Lynda and her God, who formerly had been my God, too. By grace, I was about to know that he was still my God.

Love finds me

As I heard those words being replayed in the heart and mind and soul of me that seemed to be trying desperately to turn back on again, I remember wondering why "God" – if he still was around – had not struck me dead especially with my being the "horrible" person that I was. Suddenly, the instant that thought came to me, I immediately and perhaps, miraculously…, felt consumed with the most unconditional love I could ever imagine. The consuming was ever so brief, but it was enough to give me hope. And hope, even a tiny shred, can be a wonderful, miraculous, life-transforming thing!

During November, I slowly started to feel more like me emotionally and mentally. Then, in December, the whole inflammation type picture became a bit more pronounced. Upper respiratory symptoms set in, and I lost my voice completely from around mid-December until the end of January. Then I remained very hoarse until June. As it turned out, I would not be symptom free or begin to feel anywhere near what I call my normal for a very long time.

PTSD picture emerges

I found that I could not continue writing the weekly health newspaper column I had written for years. Every time I would try to think "health or medical" thoughts my whole body would shake, and a chilling, all-consuming coldness to the bone would engulf me. I was unable to comfortably listen to friends or family when they would discuss any kind of medical procedure or illness without incurring this strange physical reaction. My body would turn freezing cold, and I would tremble violently almost like a washing machine out of balance. At one point Dr. P witnessed this at Hospital C where I had been sent for tests in the GI lab. My walking into the room – just walking into it before any procedure had even begun – had triggered what Dr. P, who had been called up from the emergency department, called "classic PTSD (post-traumatic stress disorder) symptoms."

In Search of Freedom

Still, even now at this writing, I occasionally grow cold, tremble, and get waves of nausea if someone tries to discuss serious medical problems/procedures with me. My body continues to remember every detail that my mind has tried so hard to forget. I want my body to forget. I want my mind and heart and soul to be free of the negative emotions that linger. This ongoing physical and psychological reaction is another reason I decided it would be worthwhile not only for others, but for me as well, to respond to Gwyn Hyman Rubio's request that I write the whole story.

I figured if I could truly and practically get all the negative thoughts and feelings outside of my body and mind, and onto paper that is separate from myself, then maybe I could be released from the dark clutches manufactured by the events of the fall of 2002. Perhaps I could find freedom. If not, I will have given it my best shot. Then maybe I will be able to accept the fact that some things always will trigger reactions. And when the tears come, sometimes prompted by just a smell, or a sound, or a conversation that I overhear... well, tears can be okay, too, even therapeutic.

Reviewing the Issues

In the investigation that followed my illness, when the medical records were obtained, while family and friends and some of my personal physicians were encouraging me to pursue legal action, I made an interesting discovery. Three months prior to my surgery, Hospital A had another special needs patient that I mentioned earlier. Her name had been given to me by a member of the Hospital A nursing staff. I contacted her and learned that all of her special needs were met, right down to glass IV bottles. The patient was very sensitive to plastic, vinyl, and many other things. This special needs patient told me, when I telephoned her, using contact information provided by staff at Hospital A, that she initially had been turned down by the hospital that had failed me. She said, however, that her physician went to bat for her and consulted administration. Consequently, all special needs accommodations were compassionately and competently met. Her overwhelming praise for Hospital A actually led to my first personal interest in potentially pursuing legal action. Her story only added insult to my injury. With her having been so well accommodated, it appeared that I had been discriminated against. Thus, I grew even more angry.

Lesson Learned

Communicate. Communicate. Communicate. If you or a loved one have special needs, communicate those needs clearly at all levels. Be sure you are heard. Always remember that communication is a two-way street. The speaker and the listener have equal roles in good communication.

Anger felt great compared to the depression. Feeling nothing had been the closest thing to hell that I could ever imagine. The weeks I spent in "that grey/black room where everything happened in very slow motion" as I now refer to it – a room totally void of all things that define life as being worth living – still to this day remain somewhat indescribable. I remember thinking this is where people go when life becomes too much to cope with. Maybe we turn off our hearts and souls so the body can find a way to try to survive. Maybe…

When I tried to tell Gwyn Hyman Rubio about that room she immediately knew where I had gone, and I knew that she knew. In fact, she understood perfectly. "You must tell your story," she had said. "You can help so many people." Her main character in her novel "The Woodsman's Daughter" had gone to that horrific grey/black room full of emptiness and eventually found her way back out again. That is how I knew that Gwyn knew.

During an in-depth discussion between Gwyn and me regarding the room, she very poignantly pointed out that there are those individuals who never find their way back. I knew, as she and I talked, that I wanted to become open to discovering ways to warn potential victims about such a horrific place. I also resolved to become more open to helping to find freedom for those who already have become trapped within their own personal and far too private grey and black prisons of pain and depression. At this writing, I do not know how I can or if I will actually do anything about this horror, but I am resolved to be open to finding ways to do something.

I am reminded once more, as I express my desire to "do something" of the poem I wrote nearly two decades ago, the one that provided inspiration for title of the "You Are Somebody and I am, too!" workshop in 2005:

i don't know any better
than to just go barging in
to peoples' lives
when they're hurting
'cause i've been there
and i've wondered
if somebody cared
so when i care
i try to show it
or how will they know it?
oh, sure!
i know there's always prayer
and i could just pray
that God would meet the need
and heed the cry of each aching heart
and do His part
to make it all better
and i could ask Him
to send somebody
to feed or clothe or comfort
but then
there was that time
i asked Him
to do just that for them
and He said to me
"you are Somebody"

Over time, I realized that I had developed a strange breathing pattern due to pain. I had to unlearn it. Twice, I lost most of my hair in the year following my colon surgery. I was on antibiotics for weeks following the abscess and physicians indicated that some of the complications which I had incurred during the 12 to 18 months following the surgery may have been a result of the stress, the infection, the antibiotic therapy, the very high TSH level, etc. In all honesty, the hair loss was no big deal considering so many other issues. It was just a fact.

Still, today, I have occasional obstipation issues (constipation resulting from partial blockage or obstruction in the intestines). One physician has indicated that a surgeon eventually may have to go in and cut out Dr. A's work and do either a direct connection of small bowel to rectum or a permanent ileostomy. A direct connection as described here could result in less bowel control. Where what appears to be Dr. A's attempt to build a valve or some kind of ileocecal connection of the few inches of remaining colon to the small bowel provides much better bowel control. So far, the partial blockages I have experienced have been manageable without hospitalization, because I do not panic; I just do what I have to do to cope. In fairness to Dr. A, I understand that this attempt to recreate the ileocecal valve is a great procedure and when it works, it works very well for many individuals.

In my case, I also am personally under the impression that the leakage or abscess which occurred probably originated from this area. Not only was Dr. A aware that an abscess was a possibility BEFORE she may have used sutures that would cause increased inflammation, she failed to do adequate diagnostic studies to rule out blockage or infection prior to releasing me from Hospital A. It has occurred to me and others in retrospect, that she may also have failed to do adequate pre surgery diagnostic studies. Certainly, she failed to respond appropriately to my calls on the Tuesday or Wednesday following my Monday release. Prior to surgery, she had required me to sign a paper acknowledging that leakage and abscess, among other things, were potential complications, yet I feel that she failed to even look for them. I also was told by her, before my surgery, that the seriousness of the procedure and subsequent recovery period was second only to open heart surgery. Seriousness started to take on real meaning during the days and weeks following my surgery… In fact, the word "serious" was used often on the Wednesday that I became an emergency admission to Hospital B, ten days following the colon surgery, after repeated calls to Dr. A's office during the previous 48 hours, none of which she personally returned.

My memory is quite vivid about most of the details of my Hospital A experience, but I also have documentation about the same. Within four days after my surgery, my family, and friends, who refused to leave me alone, were making notes chronicling the events that followed the surgery and treatment at Hospital A. They continued this written record at Hospital B for the remainder of the month of August. Upon my final release from Hospital B, I began making my own notes.

There are those who would suspect that legal action was first and foremost in my mind and the minds of family members at this point, since we were taking such good personal notes. That absolutely is not true, however. Good note taking is very important when serious illness is confronted. I have taught, even preached the importance of good written notes for all individuals since my early days as a nurse. In the twelve years that I published a monthly health magazine I repeatedly urged readers to keep good personal medical records, to ask for copies of everything through the years, to make good notes prior to doctor visits and to use those notes!
So, for me, note-taking is all about health and survival. That certainly is what it was about in the days and weeks following the colon surgery. Nothing else. Later, those notes would reveal that I had a good court case if I wanted to go there. Those same notes eventually showed me that I could do more to help myself and others by staying out of the judicial system.

Lesson Learned

When a patient is very ill, any family member or friend, who sits with that patient in a hospital or accompanies the patient to office visits, should take notes. Ideally, these notes should be made on a pad or in a book that remains with the patient. In such case, the patient can review the notes later when he or she feels better, in order to fully understand any instructions or data. When the patient is dependent on family or friends for ongoing support it is good for the notepad or binder to be available to all involved. This is important when even the best of care is being given. Accurate communication and accurate records of that communication is very important.

A warning for all...

This is as good a time as any, I suppose, to tell you why I no longer use phrases like "My gut tells me..." anything. I do not say phrases like "My heart breaks..." or "My head is killing me..." You see, on my third or fourth night following the removal of my colon I had a very vivid dream. It occurred while in that intermediate state between sleep and consciousness. I recall feeling like I left my body and quite fluidly glided throughout the hospital in search of my colon. In this dream, I finally found a room with containers that held various body parts and organs. I began lifting the lids on the containers in search of my colon. I desperately needed to say "Goodbye" and to thank it for all the emotional load it had carried for me over the years. This dream was a very powerful and truly unforgettable experience. It prompted me, at a later date, to do a measure of research on cell memory – a subject I still hope to revisit at some future point in time.

Missing the me I had been
Hating the me I thought I had become

I was unable to work at all until late fall 2003. Then, at or near the anniversary date of the surgery, in an act of defiance or determination or resolution to move on... or something akin to a need to get well, I accepted two small editing/publishing contract jobs. Later I would turn to my own inspirational/motivational creative writing for therapy. Early on, I just fought to find me again any way I could. I planned a high school class reunion. I reconnected with people I had not seen for years, many of whom were sufferings in ways I could not even imagine, ways that made my experiences pale in comparison. Thus, the guilt continued to mount. I remained a wimp inside. On some level, some part of me remained the little girl who had longed to curl up in a ball and so desperately wanted to disappear on that Sunday morning when my surgeon's words had seared the very essence of my soul, labeling me a whiner, a complainer, a bad nurse, an impossible patient…

A Listening Licensed Healer enters my world

In the midst of my pain, my anger, my inability to let go of the insecurity, my cold chills and trembling that would come with the mere mention of anyone's medical procedure, my anxiety, and absolute fear of ever having to trust another surgeon again… one very sensitive and brilliant medical doctor took the time to hear it ALL – not just once, but over and over again. And he also chose to take the time to listen to all that I was not saying.

Never once did he indicate that he needed to refer me to a psychologist or counselor. That he did not have time for me. That he needed to pass me on. He could have. I probably would have responded positively to any recommendation he made. In fact, I already had given psychological counseling serious consideration, but funds were limited because of so many medical bills and the extended time that I had missed from work. What this healing physician did was truly listen. Through his listening, a pathway to potential healing would become open to me.

That physician, Dr. Q, a rheumatologist, asked me at one point if I knew what it would take for me to gain closure. I informed him that "closure" was overrated, and that it was the last thing I wanted. The very fact that closure might be expected as part of some kind of legal settlement was one of many reasons that I was averse to pursuing legal action.

Among other things, I told Dr. Q that there were two desires which burned within me:

* one - protecting myself in the future

* and two - protecting others from the kind of treatment or lack thereof that I had received.

That's all that mattered for a while, and I could not see legal action as being the best way to address those issues. Many thought it was the best way, but I never did. Never, in my wildest imagination, which was not working at its best for a time, did I think, dream, or imagine that I would eventually discover ways to use what I had been through to help so many others with a much greater variety of needs. Oh, but the day would come!

Lesson Learned

Never underestimate the healing power of a good listener.

The Perfect Prescription – for me

Dr. Q gave me a verbal prescription very early in 2004. "For now, table all thoughts of legal action" he said. "You have made it clear to me and others, who think you should pursue that, that you do not want to choose such a route. I know others are pressuring you. Tell them to stop. Relinquish all such thoughts until June. At that point in time, revisit those thoughts. You will still have until mid-August, when the statute of limitations runs out, to file the lawsuit if you decide that is what you need to do to get well."

Then he asked, "What DO you think it will take for you to get well?

"My pen," I immediately answered.

He then encouraged me to use that pen to obtain healing, and to let it help me to find me again. Little did I know what an awesome journey stretched out before me as I left Dr. Q's office that day.

At some point over the preceding decade or so, my pen had become a keyboard, and so my keyboard and I became inseparable over the coming weeks and months. Pecking away at it led to my being able to expel layers and layers of anger, anxiety, fear, and insecurity. Literally, at the end of that six months I had begun to find me again and I had done it without the assistance of antidepressants or anxiety drugs.

Because of my personal medical history and long list of drug sensitivities, certain potentially helpful medications were never an option for me.

Once I realized the power of my writing, I knew I had to find a way to translate what I had done for myself into something that could be helpful to others. I knew by June of 2004, with insightful input from Dr. Q, that a workshop format would be an answer, and that legal action was out of the question. For me. I would write a self-empowerment workshop and call it: "You Are Somebody and I am, too!" It would be a personal growth program that would empower others who had been where I had been or who might someday be required by life to go there. I would try to show workshop participants how to avoid altogether that grey/black room so full of nothing or help them know how to escape from it if they ever found themselves imprisoned there.

I had wanted to get well from the start, far more than I had ever wanted to get even. Don't read me wrong – part of me wanted very much to get even. Oh yeah, big time! I am, however, a survivor, and a "get even" mindset, or negative emotions of any kind, do not serve survivors well.

For Patients and Those Who Love Them

What is in a diagnosis?

A diagnosis is a label, nothing more. For the record, as many readers may already know, a prognosis (a forecast or prediction about the outcome of a disease or the frequency with which symptoms may be expected to recur) is an opinion. Certainly, a physician's prognosis is usually a highly educated opinion, but it still is nothing more than somebody's opinion. America's present system of health care and reimbursement would collapse without all the diagnosis codes.

I will concede that diagnoses serve many purposes. A diagnosis may become something concrete on a piece of paper that may be tied to pain and symptoms that can dramatically alter one's life. A diagnosis can be a justification for some. We can look at our families or friends and say, "See, I told you how bad I was feeling. My doctor has diagnosed me with_____. I told you how sick I have been, or am." And believe me, it makes a difference whether we use the words have been, or am.

If we make our description of how bad we feel, present tense, and stick with present tense, and repeat over and over the details of our illness to anybody who will listen, as if the symptoms and pain and diagnosis and prognosis never changes… if we do that often enough, then we won't stand a chance of beating it, of dropping the label, of getting healthier... of surviving. Instead, we become the label, or even more terrifying, sometimes the label become us.

There is a difference, so I say: Down with labels altogether!

Understanding the power of a label

We should be extraordinarily cautious about the words we speak. We should be so for many reasons, but especially because we clearly can and often do BECOME them. If I say I am sick, really sick, then I am sick in a present, ongoing state of ill health. If I say I *have been* really sick, then that may or may not indicate that I am still sick, but just that little twist of wording gives me hope. "Have been" validates. It acknowledges the reality of what has been, and still may be going on, but it does not claim ongoing, continuing, controlling ownership. I don't take the words into my mind, heart, and soul quite like when I say "I am..."

Think about the power of those two words. Consider, for instance, the Old Testament story of how when God called on Moses to deliver his people from the bondage of Egypt, Moses asked God, "When I go down to my people and tell them that the God of their Fathers has sent me to set them free, what shall I tell them is His name?"

And God said to Moses "I am who I am." Some translations say, "I AM that I AM. Tell them I AM has sent me to you." Can you imagine the power of such an ever-present presence?

To my knowledge, the God of Moses is the only figure in all of history who has ever made such a publicly recorded claim of completeness and of omnipotent, ongoing power. Clearly, all the rest of us are ever-evolving. Always becoming. Changing all the time.

Consider this… In the December 2001 issue of British Medical Journal, The Lancet, Dutch cardiologist Pim van Lommel, wrote about near death experiences. When asked about consciousness and specifically, whether it was in every cell of the body, his answer was: "I think so. We know that each day 50 billion cells die." Then he points out that this extensive cell turnover means that, eventually, almost all cells that make up "me" or you" are new. And yet we don't perceive ourselves as being any different from what we always were.

This gives a whole 'nother perspective to such phrases as:

- You are what you think you are.

- You can because you think you can.

- You become what you dream you can become.

I suggest we may have far more control over the ongoing and extensive cell turnover in our bodies than we can ever imagine. I suggest that survival often is a choice. (In the upcoming book version of the "You Are Somebody..."workshop I may use the word CHOICE in the title.)

Consider also another Old Testament character named Solomon who said: "As a man thinketh in his heart, so he is." Solomon, considered by many historians to have been a very wise man also wrote: "My son give attention to my words. Incline your ear to my sayings. Do not let them depart from your sight; keep them in the midst of your heart. For they are life to those who find them, and health to all their whole body. Watch over your heart with all diligence, for from it flow the springs of life."

Did you see that? Springs of life... Say it aloud. Hear it. "Heart" in this instant is the old Hebrew word "leb" (pronounced labe) and it means literally the most internal organ, the heart... or figuratively, the feelings, the will and even the intellect, or in some instances, the center of anything.

Of course, some would ask "what, or where, is the heart of man?" And that, dear ones, that would be a topic for another book, or another lifetime. For now, I just want to say:

DO NOT EVER limit the workings of your heart, soul, mind, or will, by putting a primary focus on a diagnosis.

Not ever.

It is nothing but a label. And labels are frequently false, or at best, true only in part. The simple truth about a label is that at the one moment in time when it is applied to you, it may, in part, be accurate. From that moment on, the label begins to lose what little truth it held because you are absolutely – as you should be – and were meant to be – ever evolving, ever changing, ever growing, and always becoming.

Labels stick and remain with you only if allow them to.

Think with me about an incident from your past. Any incident. Go back to your childhood. Did you ever cry in front of other eight-year-olds? Did someone call you a cry baby? Were you? A cry baby? You cried. Yes? But you were eight years old. So you were not a baby. An hour, a day, a week later… you had learned your lesson from that crying episode. You may never have cried again in front of your peers of that period in your life. But for a brief moment or an eternity, depending on how much you accepted that label, you became the label.

Do you see what I mean?

Would you walk away from the experience of being called a cry baby and say to everyone a month later or a year later, "I am a cry baby." Of course you would not. Yet, you will walk out of the doctor's office or hospital on any given day and say to family, friends, concerned coworkers: I am a diabetic. I am an asthmatic. I am manic-depressive. I am hypertensive.

How about:

— I have been having a blood sugar problem, but we are getting it under control.

— I've been wheezing a little (or a lot) but we are working towards good management of the problem.

— I've had some episodes of energy like you would not believe, alternating with some really down times, but I'm learning how to manage.

— I've experienced some elevated blood pressure readings, but we are working to get my pressure back to within normal limits.

Avoid labels and be specific.
See the difference: "I am," "I am," "I am" versus "I have been," "I have had," "I have experienced…"
Hear the difference. "I am" is a statement of presently perceived static fact. I have been, I have had, I have experienced… indicates evolution is occurring.
Action is taking place. You are subtly acknowledging an ongoing change of status, events, or health, but

you are not announcing static, rock-solid ownership.

Don't get me wrong, sometimes ownership must happen before change or evolution can continue. Just be careful how you own anything that happens to or around you! More about that later…

And never, never, NEVER use the word victim, as in: "I'm a rape victim." "I'm a brain injury victim." "I'm an abuse victim." "I'm a breast cancer victim. "I'm a colon cancer victim." I suppose "victim" works beautifully in the courts, but in real life, it wreaks havoc. It is a horrible label. No matter what happens to you or around you, you are a victim only if you choose to be.

The Power of Words

WORDS are powerful. Hear them in the heart and soul of yourself as you read these words again:

WORDS ARE POWERFUL.

One more time and say it aloud: WORDS ARE POWERFUL.

You are what you say you are. You will become what you say you will become.

BUT sadly, you also can be what others say you are, and can become, what others say you will become.

Getting on with Life

Once you realize you are more than a diagnosis, more than a package of pain, more than a terminal disease, you can get on with your life.

I am of the opinion – no, I'm of the very deep-seated belief, that this life or this earthly existence is not all there is. It is extraordinarily important, and it is meant to be lived to the fullest. You and I are meant to experience much and learn much from all our experiences. I believe… actually, the truth is: I know with every fiber of my being that the process of experiencing life does not begin at birth and does not end with what we call death. As far as I'm concerned, both incidents, that is, our birth and death as we define them in this realm, or here on earth, are simply transition points.

I believe we come from God, and eventually return to God. I'm not sure whether we come and go from God before we finally get settled with God again at some point in eternity, but I do believe in eternity, and an eternal soul. My sisters always warn me at this point not to get too deep. They say – have said forever – that I'm too deep. Yeah, another label. I may be deep at times, but, no, I am not "too deep."

See? Once more: Fact/opinion. I, ever the survivor, get to define how fact and opinion affect me. I decide to acknowledge that I can be very deep at times, very free thinking, very open, very complex. HOWEVER, I can also be so simple, so easy, so accepting of what is, in any given present moment.

Please know that YOU, too, are so much more than any label that has ever been applied to you. Only you know the real you. Only you have the capacity to embrace and nourish the real you. No matter what your circumstances, physically, financially, psychologically, certainly spiritually, only you know the truth.

Granted, there can be times when the whole truth is hidden from your view and totally beyond your ability to grasp. That's what pain and illness can do us. Pain can really mess up our perspective. Big time! But we will have to save our pain exploration for another time or book, as well.

Let's get back to the issue of diagnosis, let me tell you of one incident that greatly impacted my life. As I already told you, in the years that I fought so hard to keep my colon, I tried a great number of measures. Some were successful for a time. But repeatedly I would feel at my wit's end, and almost be there. I want to tell you about one physician that I consulted several times during the period and who did surgery on my body at one point. (See… on my body, not on me!)

Owning all of it...

So, one day I'm in this doctor's office recounting the latest struggles, when he looks straight at me, really straight in the eye, and firmly says, "You have to own this, Mary Jane. You have to own it. Take it into yourself and own it. Then and only then will you find the answers you seek."

His words infuriated me. He was the gentlest, most trustworthy caregiver I had at the time. How dare he?

"I will not own this," I said to myself. "I will beat it or die trying."

Well, I almost did die trying, but I also beat it. Yet, he was right. I did not begin to win out over the problems, until I owned them, until they became my problems – until I assumed responsibility for my own outcome/s.

Therefore, denying a problem, a diagnosis, or label does not work either. Rational educated ownership of a problem, until you understand it and can deal with it, is a good thing. Somehow, I had walked out of that doctor's office with the notion that he had been telling me that my problem/s were me. They were mine to own and carry around with me forever, and that I could not keep coming to him or anybody else with them and expect him or them to make them go away. It took many days, and even weeks, to think through all he had said before my epiphany occurred.

Soon I realized that ownership of a problem is not a bad thing. It does not cause me to become the problem or the problem to become me. Ownership brings responsibility, and if you're lucky, the courage to do what it takes to solve the problem, or learn to live well with it, whether that means educating yourself or changing your lifestyle, having the problem surgically cut out, or just accepting certain realities. Whatever it takes to be a responsible owner of a problem is a not a bad thing; becoming that problem, letting it consume you, letting it become your label, or worse by far, letting it become you, is a very bad thing.

Caregiving Truths

As I said before, it truly disturbs me that Diagnosis has become the basis from which everything else springs. Insurance demands it to pay for health services rendered. And all those involved in treating you or your symptoms demand it so they can go by the book on the subject. Both the scary thing and a good thing about those books is that they are constantly being revised, rewritten, and changed. Be sure your professional caregiver knows about those ongoing revisions. Who knows, you yourself could be the subject of some future re-write!

So somewhere, in the midst of the search for, or even a celebration of, a diagnosis, the patient too often gets lost. A label is applied. A label that may even outlast the patient it was designed to help. While all this labeling is going on, the patient is still growing and evolving, every inch, every cell, every drop of blood. All that makes up the mind, body, soul, and spirit of the patient keeps on becoming, and far too often..., struggling alone.

Let me say here that my favorite type of health caregivers are hands-on practitioners or therapists, as in chiropractors; doctors of osteopathy, physical, occupational or massage therapists, etc. These specially trained caregivers have played a huge role in helping me find my way to health and healing on many occasions. For instance, good physical therapists must know, must practice knowing, and must somehow manage to stay aware that everything is connected. Not just the knee bone to the leg bone, or the neck bone to the backbone, but their successful practice of the art and science of medicine/healing requires an awareness of the connectedness of the body, soul and mind. For instance, anyone who has ever experienced a broken leg, or stroke, or severe burn... knows how the experience affects every area of one's life. I can't say enough about hands-on physicians, chiropractors, therapists!

For now, let me step back to the mid 1980's, and tell you about yet another a physician who was diligently working with me to get to the bottom of ongoing problems I was having at that time. So, one day, this doctor calls me at home and excitedly announces that he has found my problem. Your IGE count is 1500! He was thrilled. He said he had a diagnosis! But he had no answer for me. In reality, he never even offered a substantial diagnosis; he just had obtained some impressive blood work results. You can imagine that I was far less thrilled than he. I was still left with all the symptoms I had struggled with for years, problems that seemed to be escalating with time, and remain with me today.

But I owned what he said. I read about IGE levels, which to some extent measure your body's capacity for an allergic response. I soon recognized that I was the most allergic person that both I and my allergist had ever known at the time. Then I said, so what? Nothing was changed by that IGE level discovery or diagnosis. I suppose it became a basis for insurance approving some of the medications and treatments that I still take on a regular basis. But, so what? It was during this period that I wrote what has become one of my favorite poems:

The Label

They boxed me up and labeled me
And carefully filed me away
A neatly packaged entity to probe another day
I squirmed and fought and wiggled free
My anxious thoughts fast fading
For what they thought of me today
Seemed not worth contemplating

To a large part, I still feel exactly that way. Whenever I consult a physician, I have to go over my history. I am asked, to name all the labels I have been given over the years. And I never know how that's going to affect the service I'm seeking at any given moment. Because the doctor or health care provider to whom I am speaking may home in on any given label that I lay out for him and instantly his mind may close. I'd like to say it ain't so. I'd like to assure you that every physician on the planet sees you as a whole person every time you walk into his or her office. But I'm no fool. And don't you be one!

I may say things that you may question, but please know that I am telling you the truth as far as I, in my limited capacity, can recognize it. And the truth is that no healthcare provider or caregiver has ever, can ever, or will ever, see you as the whole person that you are. There are a few good "real" family and/or "whole person" medical or health care providers, but even they cannot grasp the whole picture. That's why you must never give over authority for your health care to anyone else. There may be times that you will choose to do a living will and appoint someone to make life and death decisions regarding artificially being kept alive and other matters. That's not what I'm talking about.

What I want you to resolve to never do is this, do not ever tell a healthcare provider or caregiver:

Here I am – figure me out – fix me!

Never do that. Stay involved.

You are your own responsibility.

Respect all who help you, then be an informed decision maker once all attainable facts are gathered. It's your body. Your life.

Better Options

What you might say is "Doctor Smith or Jones, I'm having problems in a certain area." Be as specific as you can, but be broad, too, if you need to be.

Consider saying, "I need to talk to you about these problems and learn more about what my treatment options might be." Consider wise approaches that will encourage conversation and teaching moments. Do not walk in and say "Doc, I'm hurting right here, and you've got to make it go away. You need to give me something for it. I can't stand it."

Poor doctor. With that latter approach, you have put him in the position where he has to deliver SOMETHING, or he will have failed you. And what he can deliver does not come cheap. So, he will most likely do something even when doing nothing may be the better option. He might order a barrage of tests which you may, or may not, need. He may write prescriptions for some new or tried and true drug that you may, or may not, need. He may want to give you what you ask for and expect of him and that sometimes can be very dangerous.

Now, you may really mess with his mind if you take a different approach. If you go in and tell him you want to be part of the team, even head up the team that needs to address a few problems that your body is having. Then, suddenly, your list of options is expanded.

In the first place, he's going to listen more closely. And, if you are lucky, there will be some degree of enlightening conversational exchange. He's about to learn something about you that he never knew. And he may be able to communicate things to you that you need to know.

I am personally of the opinion that no surgeon should ever cut another human being before knowing something important about them, PERSONALLY. About the only exception to that rule would be the emergency room or emergency surgery setting. In such a case, more often than not, you will have the doctor's adrenalin flowing a little more freely and that could act in your favor. You may be a John or Jane Doe on the O.R. table, but the very fact that you and your body are an emergency life and death situation heightens the surgeon's or caregiver's awareness. What I would never want to be is anybody's "routine surgery," as if there ever could be such a thing. Nothing's normal, or routine, when somebody takes a scalpel to my body!

By the way, always be sure your doctor knows all the latest developments in your physical functioning before he ever puts you under anesthesia. As I pointed out earlier, the best way to do this is to keep your own medical records or personal health file/chart. Make very concise (brief, but comprehensive) notes. Keep ongoing records of your blood pressure readings, blood work, x-ray reports, post-operative summaries, hospital discharge summaries. Ask for these records and keep them just as you would keep good service records on an automobile and have them easily accessible.

Consider that your body and your vehicle serve the purpose of transporting you from place to place. While you are not your automobile and you are not your body, either, you still need to know as much as you can about the functions of both and you need to do all you can to keep both in good working order. Just like you would be careful to use the right gasoline, oil or transmission fluids in your vehicle, you should research and know what you are putting in your body, and not just prescription or OTC medicines, but vitamins, supplements, and foods as well. Know what you are allowing into your body. Know it by name. Know the benefits and dangers.

Lesson Learned

There may be no greater tool to help the healthcare professional properly care for any patient than for the patient to have an accurate and up to date personal medical information file. In that file should be copies of any past diagnostic studies (radiology studies, lab work, etc.) surgical summaries; lists of illnesses, diseases, injuries, surgeries, allergies; and family history (the disease history of mother, father, maternal and paternal grandparents, and siblings). Such records could prove important at some time in your future. Also, patients should know the names of all medicines and supplements they take and understand why they take them. They should understand potential side effects or complications from taking them or not taking them, as well as the effect certain foods might have on the way the body uses or reacts to a medicine or supplement.

Sadly and dangerously, we research movies before we allow them into our minds better than we search drugs and food that we allow into our bodies and minds.

Wanting to be well…

At this point, I want us to consider a question Jesus Christ is reported to have once asked a very sick man. In John's gospel, the story is told of the fellow who laid by the pool daily, the pool where the "angel routinely stirred up the water giving it healing qualities." This fellow laying by the pool had been sick for 38 years. When Jesus saw him lying there, he asked him "Do you wish to get well?"

The man said to him: "Sir, I have no one to put me in the pool when the water is stirred up, but while I am coming, another steps down before me." (What a study that would make — I'd call it "Exploring the Excuses.") The question was "Do you wish to get well?" Cut and dried. Clear and simple.

Jesus appears to have overlooked the man's excuse or explanation for his ongoing circumstances. It appears that Jesus saw his heart and simply said to him, "Arise, take up your pallet and walk."

Immediately, the man did exactly that.

Am I saying that there is healing to be had for all. That it's all a matter of heart, faith, or obedience. Yes, I am. Absolutely. But bear in mind that I distinguish greatly between a healing and a curing. The crippled, disease ravaged body you may inhabit today or at some point in your life on earth, may eventually become unable to walk, or even move, but don't get the notion that the spirit within that body can't still walk, run, even soar!

I ask you to ask yourself the question, "Do I want to be well? Do I want to be healed?"

Your body may be dying. In all seriousness, despite ongoing cell renewal, our bodies actually begin dying the day we are born into this realm. I hope you all know what I mean. If your body is not presently about to quit on you, then you may have a loved one whose body has endured about all the "wear and tear" it can stand. You, or that loved one, may be getting ready to leave that body. But you can still ask yourself, "Do I want to be better?" Search your heart. Learn to know the difference between a cure and a healing. Learn well. The learning and eventual knowing may affect your eternal health.

There are no more important questions that you can ask yourself regarding your illness than "Do I want to be well, or better, or more pain free? Do I want to relinquish the mental, emotional and spiritual pain that holds me in its grasp?"

Ask it. But don't answer too quickly. Ask it. Then think about it. Think long and hard.

If your illness or pain now rules, if it and you have become one, if you do not want to live without it because of all the ways it benefits you, or don't think you can live without it because it has become you, then your answers may not be comfortable. And that's okay. You can only walk as far as the light around you lets you see the way. I know about that kind of walk and the limited light that is so often afforded us. Just remember, we are always traveling forward, evolving, growing, becoming. Always.

I often have wondered why doctors and therapists do not make that question Jesus asked a routine question on every medical history they do. Hear it again:

"Do you want to be well?"

I know that most, if not all, of us will respond affirmatively, whether we mean it or not. We may even feel insulted at being asked the question. We may even get up and walk out of the medical office of one who would dare to ask it. Hmmm, that may be the reason health care providers do not ask that question. As in "follow the money," huh?

Caring for you

We who struggle with ongoing pain and chronic illness must ask ourselves hard questions daily. Our very survival depends on our courage to ask the questions. So, ask them. Do not be afraid of the questions or the answers. Seek to know yourself well. And be kind to yourself. Be a survivor. Be more than a survivor! Care deeply for yourself. Love yourself. Even pamper yourself. Do it. To this day, I count "learn to rest and pamper yourself" among some of the best advice a doctor ever gave me. Because of all the examples set for me all my life by others, and perhaps genetically as well, I am so service oriented that it has been hard to learn to pamper myself. I have grown to enjoy the journey, however, and I look for new and special ways to do it now.

Know for sure that you have always been, are, and always will be, more than any diagnosis or label that anyone ever dares to try to stick on you. Let no man or woman, entity, theory, or so-called fact, dictate who you are, or who you are becoming.

Never focus on a limited diagnosis, or transient label.

Focus instead on becoming...

Step out in courage and faith and become, and keep on becoming, and becoming, and becoming.

And ask yourself, any time you feel like it, "What's

really in a diagnosis?"

The truth is — not much, in the grand scheme of things!

Treasures of Darkness

The fact that "You Are SOMEBODY and I am, too!" workshop attendees ask repeatedly for the story behind the program certainly has influenced me to write what you now read. During the actual workshop, I do not like to go into my own story, because I want those hours to be all about the attendees and their stories.

The fact that Gwyn Hyman Rubio inspired me to believe that writing these words would help me continue to shed lingering negative emotions certainly has further empowered me. Perhaps this little book will not only answer the questions that workshop attendees ask, but it might also further empower the reader. I can and will hope for that. In fact, I will pray for that to happen. Even now as I type these words, I pray that they will empower those who read them...

Remember, words are powerful. Words you hear, words you read, words you speak... all words are powerful! Know that fact with every fiber of your being. Be careful what words you send out into the world. Be even more careful about the words you receive into your being, your soul, into the very heart of you.

Writing the workshop was just one of several keyboard exercises among a great many that have played therapeutic roles in my life. So far, I think I only have directly tied the inspiration for the "You Are SOMEBODY and I am, too!" workshop to the defining fall and winter of 2002/2003.

As I have mentioned already, however, and you, of course, know: *way always leads on the way*. It is not likely that any of us will ever know all the reasons we do what we do. It is also not possible to know how what we do will influence the lives of others. Sometimes, we just must walk where the light falls. To adequately lay the broader and somewhat more intricate groundwork or foundation for what would become the workshop, and now, this book, I must go back in time to the mid 1980's, while I was still in nursing, and to a time when one of the earliest seeds for this work must have been sown.

One of my patients, Dr. Dwight Ike Reighard, wrote a book back then about the death of both his wife and child during childbirth. He had been devastated and his story was all about coming out of the darkness of his grief. In the front of his book, "Treasures from the Dark," Ike quoted this verse from Isaiah: "I will go before thee, and make crooked places straight; I will break in pieces the gates of brass, and cut in sunder the bars of iron; and I will give thee the treasures of darkness, and hidden riches of secret places, that thou mayest know that I, the Lord, which called thee by thy name, am the God of Israel."

That was my first personal introduction to those words. I thought they were beautiful! The passage, the book, the author's tears... and many various ways that he expressed himself back then, helped me to begin to recognize the value of the treasures of darkness and the hidden wealth of secret places. Over time, that patient/author also helped me to begin to understand that there are many, many sides to all our stories.

...

Then, in March of 1991, a few years after I had left nursing and begun a writing career, another seed was planted while I was doing a story on Southwest Christian Hospice. A terminally ill patient, who was a resident at the time, asked to see me. She wanted me to "interview" her before she died. Little could I imagine, back then, how the many sides of her story, and the countless layers of her personal truth, would forever influence my life.

...

Ten years later, more seed was sown when, during a

lazy Sunday afternoon conversation, I casually asked a friend how many times she had reinvented herself – that is, how many identities she had chosen for herself. I was not asking about her role as a daughter or a sibling. I wanted to know about vocations, relationships, activities, and the various roles she had willfully chosen in life – and how she had changed herself or evolved in order to fill those roles.

At one point in our conversation that day, I said to Betty that I thought I was living my last identity. She wisely questioned my comment. My health was not good at the time and seemed to be growing worse. I saw no way of blooming again, of becoming anything more. I was growing content, at 53..., to simply ride it out.

Her response was, "I think you probably have several more identities in you..."

I argued with her. I'd been blessed with a wonderful family, awesome friends, two great careers that had permitted me to have countless in-depth and very rewarding personal encounters with so many people who had blessed my life. I'd even had my 15 minutes of fame several times over. And finally, I had a faith I could stand on... or, at least, I thought I could.

I did not know, as my friend and I had our discussion about our various identities, that I was about to start a three year journey which would briefly take me into the depths of depression, rob me of all self-esteem for a time, and test my faith like it had never been tested, before I would come back around to being me again – not just the me I had been prior to that conversation, but a much wiser, more courageous me, with a stronger purpose than I had ever known, or even imagined... before I went into the grey-black darkness of my soul and was forced to go exploring for treasure in the hidden places of my own heart.

Once one decides he or she wants to survive and is willing to do what it takes to survive, then it's just a matter of making the journey. Please know I have seen many people whose bodies have died while their spirits have soared during such a journey – a journey that requires great courage and takes us into the heights and depths of our eternal existence. I, who had lost all self-confidence during my ordeal, picked up my pen and began to discover that I was still somebody, somebody special, somebody worthy of making a comeback, of finding me, and fully being me again!

As I traveled deeply into the darkness of my existence and started to record what I found there, eventually beautiful things began to show up on my paper: treasure of darkness is what I discovered.

Once I realized what I had found, I started to look for positive ways to use or share the riches I had unearthed. Soon, I made the most amazing discovery:

I realized that treasure was mine to keep. Shortly after that revelation, I realized I just needed to try to show others how to make their own journeys, discover their own treasure, and learn how to use it to make a difference every day in their own lives and in the lives of others. Thus, the foundation for the You Are SOMEBODY and I am, too! workshop began to make itself known to me.

Hope

I often have written and spoken about HOPE since I witnessed my first "DOA" (dead on arrival) suicide as a hospital nursing assistant at age 18; thus, hope is a theme of much of my writing. Beyond that theme, whether I am writing a newspaper column, a work of fiction or non-fiction, a feature story, or poetry, I am consistently true to a distinctive and healing southern voice. Readers and listeners tell me I have learned to speak and write from a heart that knows how to touch (and challenge...) the heart of a wide range of audiences. I hope they are right. I will agree that it is all about heart with me. I like it that way. I am blessed.

The foundations of my books, columns, talks, and programs can be traced in part to family and faith... and to wonderful and rewarding relationships with so many former patients who taught me much about the "pain behind the pain," as well as the joy that makes the pain bearable.

Throughout my second career as a writer, literally thousands of individuals have continued to teach me as I have been invited to interact with them on so many levels where hearts speak freely.

Many influential and very special "somebodies" have shared with me valuable insight about true hope and happiness. Repeatedly, they have demonstrated the power of choice, imagination, dreams, forgiveness, and love as they have allowed me to watch them redefine success and healing along their own unique and very personal journeys. I have been so extraordinarily blessed as I have shared these journeys. It is my duty to continue the sharing.

I Am SOMEBODY!

In 2004, I had 750 copies published of a book containing a collection of some of the columns I had written over the previous 18 years. I chose to title that collection "You Are Somebody and I am, too!" based on the following poem which I shared with you earlier and will repeat again here for your convenience:

you are Somebody

i don't know any better
than to just go barging in
to peoples' lives
when they're hurting
'cause i've been there
and i've wondered
if somebody cared
so when i care
i try to show it
or how will they know it?
oh, sure!
i know there's always prayer
and i could just pray
that God would meet the need
and heed the cry of each aching heart
and do His part
to make it all better
and i could ask Him
to send somebody
to feed or clothe or comfort
but then
there was that time
i asked Him
to do just that for them
and He said to me

"you are Somebody"

You and Yours / Me and Mine

In closing that 2004 column collection I wrote a few words that directly helped to lay the groundwork for what would become the workshop by the same name. I share that closing with you here:

As I apply the last bit of editing to this collection of columns pulled from among nearly a thousand that I have written since 1986, I do so with mixed feelings. When I changed careers in 1986 and left my job as a nurse to try my hand as a writer/publisher, little did I know all the ways I would be permitted to continue to take the pulse of the people. It has been my privilege to not only take the pulse, but to almost touch the beating hearts of so many people with whom I have interacted over the years. To pick one person, or even make a short list of persons, who have most influenced me with the rhythms of their lives would be impossible. I can say but one thing with absolute certainty to all whose paths have crossed mine:

You and yours have touched the lives of me and mine

and we are changed forever.

Thus, it is in life. We touch one another daily, hourly, moment by moment. I suspect when it comes right down to it, life may actually be measured in seconds: the seconds that it takes to smile, wink, laugh, give a hug, whisper a prayer, offer encouragement. Nothing is ever as complicated as we try to make it. It is enough that we live and love well. And what would be the secret to accomplishing that? Ah, to live well, that's easy — all we have to do is do what only we can do and do it with all our might.

Did you know that the "do unto others as you would have them do unto you" theme of the Christian faith manifests itself in every major religion? It may be worded differently, like "what you send out into the lives of others comes back into your own," but it's there. To some extent, every faith teaches us to treat others the way we want to be treated. When we seek to love others the way we love ourselves, then you and yours, me and mine… we start to become one. The world will be a better place when we resolve to base our actions on that one common principle. To recognize the theme is a beginning. With such recognition must come a willingness to act. With you and yours, and me and mine, working together, there will be no limit to what we can accomplish. Ah, what a glorious adventure it is that awaits those willing to work together to do what only we can do.

Until later,

Mary Jane Holt

March 15, 2004

Following those few words, I ended that little collection of columns with this poem:

What Only You Can Do

"and leave undone forever what only you can do"
words which haunt me ever
as daily I am pulled tossed to and fro
always on the go
demands here … expectations there
so I stand still...
though I want to move to somewhere
but where is somewhere?
and why must I go there?
there is so much I want to do, to say someday
but when is someday?
and will I know it when it comes?
direction is unclear
a low and winding road beckons
a lovely valley lies below
the ocean calls, the mountains, too
and oh! how I want to go!
but yon path looks smooth and straight...
so, I linger here to await
a word from You
to join the crowd seems right
when "they say" we can win if I join the fight
and perhaps we could win a battle, maybe two
but war will wage on
and what will it all matter
when I face You
if I have left undone forever
what only I could do?

Thus, the "You Are SOMEBODY and I am, too!" workshop, born of the experiences described herein and written "as only I can write it," takes workshop attendees into deep corners of their hearts, shines for them a revealing light on their own magnificent treasures of darkness found there, then brings them back to an "attitude of gratitude – no matter what…" and equips them with newfound power, purpose and promise for the future. Some attendees are softened. Others tell me they are broken. Many describe themselves as rejuvenated, inspired, motivated. All claim to be blessed. For such response I am so very thankful.

There are circumstances that we all go through which we perceive at the time to be very "bad." We often suck it up and resolve to just try to get through such situations any way we can. When the trying or painful time is past, we then tuck away the experience, or at least the emotions it evoked, and, sometimes, even all conscious memory of it, into some corner of our heart. There we build a safe wall around it. To protect ourselves, we say. The trouble is, that wall becomes a barrier that also protects us from learning all we could have learned from such experiences.

The events of the fall and winter of 2002/2003 will never be forgotten. Without a doubt, that period held many defining moments for my life. During those long months of pain, many things happened about which I can do absolutely nothing now. There is, however, no limit to what I can do with what I have learned, and with all the ways I have been blessed to keep living and growing and becoming. Forgiveness has come slowly, but it finally has come. For that I am deeply thankful.

Hating Dr. A for so long for all the ways I felt that she failed me required much soul searching on my part. The soul searching has been good for me. Had the choice been mine to make, would I have chosen the path that took me into that horrific dark grey valley of hatred and anger and depression?

Absolutely not!

Have I now come to feel truly thankful for all things that have brought me to this day, this moment, this freedom to tell my story with a prayer that others will be helped, blessed, inspired, motivated – perhaps healed? Oh, yeah, I am indeed thankful, so very thankful…

I wrote the "You Are Somebody and I am, too!" workshop for adults. My initial intended audience was the healthcare professional who is so prone to burnout. Little did I know I was putting together a program that would benefit people of all ages, and from all walks of life. There is constant amazement on my part at how differently the workshop has been perceived by all who attend. Early on, I was asked if the program would be appropriate for young people, and I said no. I was so wrong!

Feedback from participants who attended the first PILOT "You Are Somebody and I am, too"! Workshop for Youth as presented on July, 2005, at a Boys and Girls Club of America Teen Center provided that. Ten youth, between the ages of 12 and 15, attended. All ten turned in feedback. It appeared to both me and their director, that I did actually have the wholehearted attention of all ten participants throughout the five-hour program. It was amazing!

All youth were very demonstrative with their appreciation for the workshop. All told me thank you. All of them hugged me… and enthusiastically expressed their appreciation in other ways. All of them established a little place for themselves in my heart. Their attention, enthusiasm and responses mirrored that of adults who would eventually experience the program. I knew while being held in the embrace of this awesome group of youngsters that I had done something right with what I had perceived for a long time to be a very wrong chain of events. Suddenly, I was consumed with gratitude for all things… literally ALL things – since all roads had led me to this place and to the awesome privilege of being accepted into the hearts of these very special young people.

As I think back over the physical and emotional embraces of those teens, I realize how much easier they made it for me from that day forth to choose to own it all — all that the experiences my earth journey had afforded me to date... and to be thankful on some level for each and every experience.

In the same sense, I still feel a deep gratitude to Gwyn Hyman Rubio for the emotional and intellectual embrace she gave me on October 16, 2005.

Strangely, just a few days after my lengthy conversation with Gwyn, I had a similar interaction with Attorney Charles Pyke. Charles, who wisely and efficiently specializes in estate planning, probate, trust administration and elder law issues, was also a very influential and highly respected member of Southwest Christian Care's Board of Directors at the time. He had just observed my workshop for the first time and when he finished, he turned to me and said, "You would do it all over again in a heartbeat, wouldn't you?"

"Heavens No!" I gasped.

"Sure you would. You would choose it all over again knowing now what wonderful blessings have come out of it — knowing all the people who have been and can be inspired and helped and..."

"No," I interrupted him and repeated, "I absolutely would not ever have chosen this road and would certainly not choose it again."

I don't think he believed me. Later, within hours, I began to question my earlier protests. As it turns out, by the end of the day, I had begun to wonder if I myself believed me.

I went into the valley in 2002. I was well on my way out of it in 2005 at this writing. The workshop about which people have had such good things to say may be an awesome experience for them. For me, it has been the hardest and most painfully challenging work I have ever done. The valley has been a long one. Oh, I finally can glimpse the mountain every now and then. It's out there. And when I am finally on top of it – and I will be – I will look back once more and better understand "where God has brought me from and where I could have been…" Perhaps then I will more readily say, "Yes, I would have chosen it." That would be wonderful. I think I will look forward to that day. Charles is probably right. I think it might be a comin'!

Continuing the journey…

In a conversation with Dr. Q, on October 6, 2005, I said I may have come up with the answer – with a way to help rid the courts of frivolous lawsuits that do more harm than good for all involved. Patients need an easily accessible system whereby they can report directly on their physicians, hospitals, nursing homes, and other healthcare facilities. Those physicians deserving of high marks would get them. Those deserving of failing grades would get those. Patients could feel proud to share their good experiences. They could feel somewhat vindicated at having a way to record and share their bad experiences. I'm talking about a national physician report card here that would be available to all. Give me that and I, personally, will never talk punitive damages or pain and suffering again. It is not reasonable to expect a mistreated patient to walk away from his or her mistreatment without some means of seeking justice, fairness, or even vindication.

In cases where people are injured and medical bills must be paid, ongoing care or therapy is necessary, or when a person is deprived of the ability to productively work and earn an income, then certainly these issues should be addressed in the courts whenever possible. "Pain and suffering" however, is a very subjective phrase. In early talks with attorneys, when I diligently sought to explore all responsive options concerning the way I had been treated, and had not been treated, I was amazed that there were attorneys who felt they could not work with me if I was "so determined to get well and strive for a positive attitude." Seriously, they said that! For sure, in their eyes, I simply was not the perfect "victim." It was explained to me that such a positive outlook as mine "would not serve *us* well in court."

In retrospect, the easy way for Hospital A, Dr. A and I to attempt to reach some kind of settlement and the ever so highly recommended "closure" regarding my proper treatment and/or lack thereof may have been to play the game right and make my way through the courts.

Like I said earlier, however, closure is way overrated. I am just not sure how that word has come to be such a big deal. I am convinced that an open-door policy for the soul is the only way for me to live. I want to be free to come and go at will along all the past, present and future avenues of my life. I choose the freedom to revisit past experiences whenever I need a missing puzzle piece, or whenever some new revelation comes my way that I want to celebrate in its entirety. Paradigm shifts or epiphanies are always enhanced when we are privy to the big picture. I just don't think "closure" would serve me well, since I always seek and am ever open, ready, even eager, to catch a glimpse of that big picture any chance I get.

I may never totally figure out how Dr. A's words could have so severely wounded my spirit on that Sunday morning in 2002. I only know that they did. That knowledge assures me that none of us are immune to such damage. I am a strong willed, assertive person; but such attributes started to fade into nothingness on that Sunday August morning as the pathetic child in pain within me started to curl up into a helpless ball of lonely grey anguish.

Maybe I had waited too long to agree to the surgery and allowed the symptoms I had tried to manage for so many years to wear me down. Maybe Dr. A was the one who had been worn down by personal issues in her own life. Maybe I was a poor communicator after having tried to put up a good front for so long. Maybe Dr. A just did not like me and she had managed to hide it up until that Sunday morning. Maybe she had used the wrong suture on me, as hospital records indicate may have been the case, and had been putting up a defense all week because of that. Maybe none of this speculation on my part matters.

Perhaps such searching exercises will never lead to the insights that I seek. Asking, seeking, desiring to better understand many things is part of the life pattern I have chosen. It is my custom, simply my way to ask the how and why of things whenever I feel that I should. I long to understand. To see the big picture. Every now and then I catch a glimpse of it. Sometimes, I finally get it. Sometimes, I do not. I do feel that I am closer now than I have been in a very long time to catching a glimpse of that bigger picture.

The experiences I have shared with you have led me to believe that all of us are potentially only one heartbeat away from being damaged, injured, hurt, sometimes beyond repair… by the callousness, negligence, or potentially wounding words or actions of a few others. Any one of us is only a breath away from having our self-confidence shaken by the actions or deeds of others. Personal and professional identities and the income that go with them can be gone in an instant. Loved ones, with or without warning, can be taken from us. Physical illness, injury, mental anguish, emotional trauma, and spiritual battles abound. Sudden or chronic abuse of any kind can send us spiraling and can bring us to the brink…

From the brink of depression and despair I am convinced one can choose to reach up and out. Questions should be asked. It is important to seek needed help. Not all who seek can find, but very few will find who do not seek. With the seeking comes the opportunity to reach out and take peace and take joy and take a reason to go on living and loving, and caring for and about yourself and others. Such opportunities come even when we do not find that which we think we seek.

I am still not as well as I want to be emotionally, but I am getting there. My legs still grow weak, and I get very cold, tremble and occasionally have waves of nausea if someone tries to talk to me about a medical/surgical procedure they experienced. This is something new and strange to me. PTSD has taken on a brand-new meaning! Throughout 18 years of nursing, I do not ever recall experiencing such a reaction either in the clinical setting or outside of it. Occasionally, I will talk aloud about my Hospital A experiences to a very few family members and friends in a continuing effort to dilute my memory of the experience. To filter out the negative impact. To diminish undesirable physiological reactions that linger.

Repeatedly, the symptoms I describe have recurred while working on this manuscript. The tears still come. During the early part of 2003, I felt ashamed of such weakness and disappointed in myself. I even thought of myself as a wimp for a time. I no longer do that. More and more I am growing proud of myself, thankful for who I have been, who I am, and who I am becoming. I am a survivor. Always have been. Always will be.

I am, however, MUCH MORE than a survivor. The survivor in me might would have and perhaps should have chosen, very early on, to just drop this entire story, forget it, put it into some corner of my heart and build a wall around it. Even legal action could have been a viable option for just the survivor side of me.

As I told you earlier, however, I also am a patient advocate. Born and bred almost from birth to stand up for the less fortunate, for others in need, for those without a voice. I mentioned earlier that such a trait has landed me in more than one precarious position over the years. It also has afforded me the most amazing blessings! I must believe that this attempt to share my story will benefit others. I choose to believe that some element of what I have recorded will encourage patients to be better patients, nurses to be better nurses, and doctors to be better doctors. It was for the benefit of others who would follow after me that I could not just drop any of this. I trust now that my words will fall into hearts in need of the Lessons I hope I have been able to share effectively.

Oh! One more thing I don't think I have told you. Many months after my ordeal at Hospital A and well before the statute of limitations was up for me to be able to sue, I wrote a 12 page letter to the administrator of that hospital and hand delivered it. I insisted that he read it aloud in front of me. Then I left with a fervent prayer in my heart that he would act on what I had given him. A few years afterwards I met a couple at an event who looked at my name tag and said, "Your name sounds familiar." I asked where they worked. He was in upper management, and she was a nurse at Hospital A. During that encounter, I learned that the administrator had indeed acted on the suggestions I made in my letter.

I'm not saying legal action is never the right way when one is harmed by the negligence of others. I am just saying there are other more healing and perhaps wiser ways to address issues.

Final Lessons Learned

Prior to 2002, I had been in position as a nurse, as a family member, and as a friend, to sympathize with various individuals, to encourage them, to run interference for them, to seek for better understanding between them and their health care providers. My sympathy was strong; therefore, sometimes my efforts were successful.

Then it came my turn, while in a sick, weakened, and debilitated state of body, to personally hear words too hastily spoken and far too ill chosen – words that damaged the heart and soul inside of the body I wanted so desperately to make well again.

Now, I truly empathize with patients like never before. There is a huge difference in what one would or might say or do when one sympathizes, compared to what one becomes willing to do when one truly can empathize. That difference is why I write such a personal memoir as this.

The ultimate lesson I have learned: Sometimes, an individual just may be meant to walk a certain path to get from Point A to Point B, or C, or D... and thus be able to accomplish that which only he or she can accomplish along a journey which only he or she can make.

As my personal journey continues, I find that forgiveness, which has come long and hard, now is in order for all those I have hated and blamed for my own pain, as well as for the pain of so many other patients whose quiet, submissive tears I have seen fall over the years. Perhaps some force much bigger than anything I ever could attempt to describe has been at work all along.

AND NOW…

Before you read on, I want you to know that what you are about to read came to me several days after I finished writing what you have read up until this point. When I wrote on the previous page, "Perhaps some force way bigger than anything I ever could attempt to describe has been at work all along," I thought that line would be a great way to end this writing project. Little did I know what kind of revelation was in store for me! Talk about catching a glimpse of the big picture! You gotta be tough if that kind of insight is truly the desire of your heart. You gotta be real tough, or know Someone who is, on Whom you can lean. I do a lot of leaning.

Now, you can read on…

One last powerful revelation…

Many years ago, when I was still actively nursing, I made an early morning decision that, for a time, I came to believe may have indirectly cost a patient his life. I did not make a phone call that I wanted to make on that patient's behalf, because everybody all around me did not want me to make the call. All other staff in the shared setting felt that adequate professional help was in the building at that time. I gave in to peer pressure. Against my better judgment, in every sense of the word, and yes, against even my own little inner voice – the voice I did not listen to all the time back then – I gave in to the wishes of others and called in the wrong physician to "care" for the man in need.

The man's needs were not met, and he died a painful death as that day neared its close. I came to realize later that he most likely would have died anyway. Even if I had called in the physician that I knew was the better choice, death probably would have come. It would not have come so painfully, however. This I know. If I had followed my heart, instead of protocol, that dear patient would not have died with his wife, son, and he himself, wondering why no one was doing anything to try to help. That family would not have felt totally deserted in a long and lonely hall at a large, reputable hospital.

I have never forgotten that experience. Will never

forget it. Cannot forget. And for many long years, I could not forgive myself. Since early childhood, well before I ever knew what advocate meant, much less "patient advocate," I have been one. I knew what was best for that patient. I just did not do it. A personal sense of professional belonging, and what a few people whose opinion of me I wrongly thought was important, mattered more.

Then.

My life was changed forever that day. I did not want it to be changed. I loved my life. I cherished my identity at that moment. I enjoyed my place of service. I would go back in time in a heartbeat and undo the events of that morning if I could.

I cannot.

Today, I still live with a very painful memory, and with the awareness that I must never allow what other people think of me to influence my actions when I know the right thing to do in any given situation. The dilemma I face – that we all face – is "how do we know what is the right thing to do?"

It is a hard question. Hard answers often come slowly to hard questions – if they come at all. Sometimes we just have to wing it. We have to walk by faith until we have some awareness that we made the right choice, said the right thing, or made the right move.

Sometimes we just must walk by faith because "until…" never comes.

There is no doubt that my action, or inaction, on the morning that I just told you about has influenced every day of my life since then. Did it change my calling in life? No. Did it reinforce it? Like you cannot imagine.

I often have wondered if so much of what I have done since that fateful day has been part of an effort to do penance, to make amends, to demonstrate how sorry I am and to show how much I want to make a difference. Was that day the reason I launched the little community health magazine that I published for 12 years? Is that day the reason I stand up for others now and fight like never before?

Did I accept what Dr. A said that Sunday morning into my soul, my heart, and even my entire being because I felt on some level that I deserved to hear it? Had I been waiting for years for somebody to tell me aloud… what I knew in my heart: that I was a horrible nurse?

When Dr. A said, "You are just like all my other nurse patients. Nurses are horrible patients…" I heard "nurse," I heard "patients," and I heard "horrible." Not only had I labeled myself a horrible nurse on that fateful day so many years earlier when I had failed to go against protocol and do in my heart what I knew was best for my patient, suddenly I was a horrible nurse patient, as well.

Only now, as I put the finishing touches on this manuscript, do I realize that everything those three words had ever meant to me may have come flooding back into my unconscious mind on that Sunday morning when Dr. A verbalized her distorted judgment.

Until now I had never connected the two events.

Yet there I was and had been for a full week, asking for compassionate, competent medical care that was not administered. I was in a hospital and under the care of health professionals I thought I could trust to provide such. They failed me. Perhaps, they failed me like I had indirectly failed my patient years earlier...

On some unconscious level, did I receive Dr. A's words and allow them to do the damage they did because I felt I deserved them?

I find some comfort at this point as I remember and connect. The big picture is bearable. I sense that a measure of peace is settling gently into some corner of my heart where I feel I can now tenderly tuck away many aspects of this, my story, in part.

Until now, I have been unable to understand how Dr. A's words could have done so much damage. So, now that I am gaining a better understanding, I ask myself: Can I drop it now? Can I let it go? Can I forget those words that still ring in my heart?

"You are just like all my other nurse patients. Nurses are horrible patients. You think you have to tell us what to do. I am the doctor and you are the patient. You are supposed to tell me how you feel, not what to do. I decide that."

Can I forget? My response is: Absolutely not. I refuse to forget. Why?

* BECAUSE I am a strong, very assertive personality. A fighter. A survivor.

* BECAUSE I was a good nurse, am a good nurse, and always will be a good nurse.

* BECAUSE I am an educated patient who takes responsibility and pursues good health.

Since I am all of this and more, and since I know there are so many people who are not as strong, assertive, or educated, I do not forget. I must not forget. I choose to speak out and I write. I educate and defend.

And I remember:
Words heal. Words kill.
They heal and kill the mind, body, spirit of us all. The most valuable healthcare professional regularly uses words that heal, encourage, educate, and/or

demonstrates some degree of competent compassion. For any doctor, nurse, nursing assistant, or therapist… ANY healthCARE professional to deliberately use words that hurt, discourage, criticize, and further debilitate a vulnerable patient is totally unacceptable.

As painful as silence can be, it is often better than saying the wrong thing. There are those who would disagree with that statement. I would suggest that any communication is better than no communication between two reasonably mentally and physically healthy individuals. There are occasions, however, when silence is not only better, but also much preferred. It is so much better for a weak, debilitated and totally dependent patient to think a healthcare provider might not care than for that provider, on a bad day or in a weak moment, to open his mouth and let fly a series of ill-chosen words that "prove" to the patient that he does not care.

I find it shocking that until now I had never connected the two events. I know that present painful life experiences are often compounded by past painful life experiences. For instance, the grief we felt when our puppy died at age seven, the grief we felt when our best friend moved away at age 15, the grief we felt when a longtime neighbor was killed in an auto accident ten years earlier… it all comes back to us when a parent dies. Or a child. Or a close friend.

Consciously, subconsciously, unconsciously, we remember, and we connect all things. Sooner or later that big picture comes into focus. The grief, the joy, the pain, the ecstasy, all the perceived successes and failures... all of it is there in that big picture that I so like to catch a glimpse of every now and then.

Remember how I told you I chose to leave nursing in 1986 because I wanted to write. At first, it really was just going to be a sabbatical. I said I needed to write to heal a few emotional wounds I was carrying at the time and that my intentions were to return to the clinical setting within six months, a year at most. Now you know the source to some degree of those old emotional wounds.

As these words appear before me, I am more thankful than ever before that way leads to way, and that I never went back. There is no bypassing Points B, C, D, E, F and G to get to H or Z. And sooner or later we realize there is no going back to Point A. Life is what it is. It has been a long journey to this point in time where this ever so elusive glimpse of the big picture has been presented to me for yet another ever so brief viewing.

I am perceived my some, perhaps by many... to be a woman of great faith. It is not an accurate perception. Faith comes hard for me. What faith I have is almost a direct result of being permitted to catch my occasional glimpses of the big picture that I so hunger to see from time to time. What you have read up until this point may lead you to think since I am a (re)searcher, since I ask so many questions, since I seek so long and hard to know and to understand... that it is I who makes this picture come together. Certainly, you may think that. Shucks, I have even thought that a time or two. But I know better.

"Perhaps some force way bigger than anything I ever could attempt to describe has been at work all along," is a good thought to leave with you. I am convinced that there is indeed a Force or Power at work in all our lives that influences us. It guides us. It inspires us. It shines Directional Light. My deep and growing awareness of that Force tells me this and more.

In closing...

By grace, for the better part of my entire life, I have chosen to walk a path where what "they" think and say can still hurt from time to time; but what "they" say seldom sways me now. The truth is that "they" often will forget what they have said. They may even forget immediately after their careless words have left their lips, while you or I are left to live forever with the poor decisions we make based on our foolish acceptance as truth what "they" said to or about us. After I wrote and started presenting the "You Are Somebody and I am, too!" self-empowerment workshop, I was prepared for the content to cause some people to judge me harshly and perhaps criticize my efforts to raise awareness or consciousness. You know what? I figured that was okay. In fact, it was SO okay. I am proud of, and so thankful for, the contents of that workshop. It empowers. It strengthens. It encourages. It offers guidance. Numerous people have told me that the workshop has redirected their lives. It certainly has given added direction to mine. Finally, I am beginning to understand many things that Rick Warren wrote about in "The Purpose Driven Life." Oddly, contrary to the criticism I expected, people invariably respond so positively that I am simply left in awe. The workshop is all about choices, consequences, personal responsibility, life-changing attitudes and so much more. These are things I know about. And so I write, and speak, and walk by grace and a growing faith, wherever my path might lead. It is not always an easy path; it is, however, my chosen path and I walk it in gratitude as the Directional Light that falls upon it shows me how to make my way.

Thursday, October 20, 2005

Dear Doctor:

    I forgive you… and I forgive me, too.

~ MJH

Tuesday, August 24, 2021

Dear Nurse,

I'm extraordinarily proud of 99.99 percent of you and so very thankful that you, with me, can say:

"Dear Doctor, I am your teacher."

~ MJH

September, 2021

As we prepare to print this book it is with a sincer
God will sustain the many nurses who want to give
walk away as they enter their 19th month of Caring
Patients with other hospital acquired infections on t
again.
These same nurses long to take an extra juice to a p
again; to smile as they fluff a pillow; to have time to
patient's sore, aching back; to enjoy a meaningful be
with a lonely patient … but they can't.
It's taking all they can do just to keep their patients
breathing during their exhausting 12-hour plus shifts
When they leave the hospital, they cry. They go home.
strip. They bathe. They hug their loved ones.
And sometimes they don't go back.
We need them to go back.

And so we pray… We pray like our lives could depen
their going back.

~ mjh

Mary Jane Holt, a retired nurse, wrote
an award-winning newspaper column for 25 years and
published a community health magazine for 12 years
before transitioning into broadcast journalism.

OTHER BOOKS

From the Corners of my Heart
What IS Love?
MALIGNANT EMOTION
You Are Somebody and I am, too
BRAZILBILLY, The JesseLee Jones Story
SOUL FOOD and Spirit Vittles, *Volume One*
SOUL FOOD and Spirit Vittles, *Volume Two*
Those Moments That Matter

Made in the USA
Coppell, TX
07 February 2022

73076119R00105

Thursday, October 20, 2005

Dear Doctor:

I forgive you... and I forgive me, too.

~ MJH

Tuesday, August 24, 2021

Dear Nurse,

I'm extraordinarily proud of 99.99 percent of you and so very thankful that you, with me, can say:

"Dear Doctor, I am your teacher."

~ MJH

Dear Doctor, I am your teacher…

September, 2021

As we prepare to print this book it is with a sincere prayer that God will sustain the many nurses who want to give up and walk away as they enter their 19th month of Caring for Covid Patients with other hospital acquired infections on the rise again.

These same nurses long to take an extra juice to a patient again; to smile as they fluff a pillow; to have time to rub a patient's sore, aching back; to enjoy a meaningful bedside chat with a lonely patient … but they can't.

It's taking all they can do just to keep their patients alive and breathing during their exhausting 12-hour plus shifts.

When they leave the hospital, they cry. They go home. They strip. They bathe. They hug their loved ones.

And sometimes they don't go back.

We need them to go back.

And so we pray… We pray like our lives could depend on their going back.

~ mjh

Mary Jane Holt, a retired nurse, wrote
an award-winning newspaper column for 25 years and
published a community health magazine for 12 years
before transitioning into broadcast journalism.

OTHER BOOKS

From the Corners of my Heart
What IS Love?
MALIGNANT EMOTION
You Are Somebody and I am, too
BRAZILBILLY, The JesseLee Jones Story
SOUL FOOD and Spirit Vittles, *Volume One*
SOUL FOOD and Spirit Vittles, *Volume Two*
Those Moments That Matter

Made in the USA
Coppell, TX
07 February 2022

73076119R00105